MAGNET SCHOOLS

Magnet School Conference Series Number I

NOLAN ESTES *and* DONALD R. WALDRIP,
Editors

First Annual International Conference on Magnet Schools

Dallas, Texas   March 9 to 12, 1977

Sponsors:
The American Association of School Administrators
The National School Boards Association
The Council of the Great City Schools
Department of HEW, Dallas Regional Office
Texas Education Agency, Region 10 Educational
    Service Center

Conference Host:
Nolan Estes, Superintendent, Dallas Independent
    School District, Dallas, Texas

Conference Coordinator:
Donald R. Waldrip, Educational Consultant,
    Cincinnati, Ohio

MAGNET SCHOOLS

Legal and Practical Implications

Edited by

NOLAN ESTES and DONALD R. WALDRIP

New Century Education Corporation

Standard Book Number: 0-8329-0001-X
Library of Congress Number: 77-94166

Published 1978 by
NEW CENTURY EDUCATION CORPORATION
275 Old New Brunswick Road, Piscataway, New Jersey 08854

Printed in the United States of America

Table of Contents

DR. NOLAN ESTES is superintendent of the Dallas Independent School
District, Dallas, Texas, and was host of the First International Magnet
School Conference in March of 1977.

DR. MARIO D. FANTINI, Dean of Education, University of
Massachusetts, is the author of Alternative Education: A Sourcebook for
Parents, Teachers, Students, and Administrators, and Public Schools of
Choice.

THE HONORABLE JOHN GLENN, U.S. Senator from the State of Ohio,
is the sponsor of the School Innovation Integration Act, enacted last fall as
PL-94-482.

DR. B. FRANK BROWN is the Director of the National Commission on
Youth (established by the Charles F. Kettering Foundation, through its
educational affiliate, the Institute for Development of Educational
Activities, Inc., [I/D/E/A], Melbourne, Florida).

DR. JOHN B. DAVIS, JR., President of Macalester College, St. Paul,
Minnesota, formerly was superintendent of Minneapolis Public Schools
(1966-1975).

MS. MARGE HOLS is an educational writer who has been under contract
to the Minneapolis public schools since 1972.

MS. GAIL GRAFFLIN FULLINGTON, formerly on the staff of the Dallas
Independent School District, and now completing her Ph.D. at the
University of Oregon, is the recipient of the South Dakota Shankland
Memorial Scholarship for Advanced Study in Educational Administration.

DR. DONALD R. WALDRIP was superintendent of schools in Cincinnati,
Ohio (1972-1976), and is now an educational consultant and president of
Don Waldrip and Associates, Cincinnati, Ohio, a consulting firm
specializing in the development and implementation of alternative systems.

MR. EDGAR J. LOTSPEICH, who has a varied background in public
administration and human relations, is a parent of children who attend
Cincinnati alternatives.

Acknowledgements

The editors are indebted to the contributors to this book, who made the First Annual International Conference on Magnet Schools such a significant meeting, and to the Dallas Independent School System for hosting the conference. The editors also express their appreciation to Leona Abraham for the excellent preparation of the manuscript for publication.

Special thanks go to Ceil Cleveland Waldrip for her editorial assistance.

MAGNET SCHOOLS

Introduction

The First Annual International Conference on Magnet Schools was held in Dallas in the spring of 1977 to broaden understanding of, and sharpen insights into, an educational concept which has proved successful in the past under different names. The concept of the Magnet School is not new in itself, but the application of the concept has been expanded and modified over the years as the needs of students in our society have changed.

The first "magnet" high school in Dallas began in 1929—nearly a half-century ago—in the form of a technical trade school. Students from throughout the Dallas Independent School District could request to be transferred there. The program was geared to the student who would end his education with high school graduation; and skill acquisition, mainly in the trades, was the goal of students who elected to attend the program. This school continued to function until it was closed in 1971 under a federal court order.

The next "magnet" school in Dallas came into being in the form of the Metropolitan Alternative School, a school for students who, for one reason or another, did not function well in a regular setting. These students included dropouts who had dropped back in, potential dropouts, students with financial and family problems, third-party assignments from the Student Affairs office, or those who simply had a problem adjusting to the structure of the regular school setting. The program started in 1970, with one teacher and eight students, in an old abandoned lumber company building. It has grown to include five metro schools located in different areas of the city. Students are allowed to pursue study at their own pace with work assigned on an individual basis. The amount of time each student spends, and the number of weeks required to complete a course of study, vary according to the needs or work schedules of the students. Some of the students attend full-time; others are part-time workers and part-time students.

A third type of Magnet concept was begun in 1971 when the $21 million Skyline Career Development Center opened with a voluntary student body drawn from every high school in Dallas. Youngsters selected a career field or "cluster" from twenty-eight possible choices and spent half of each school day studying in their chosen field. Choices ranged from architectural design and aeronautics to the world of construction and advanced science.

The main difference in approach between Skyline and the technical high school is that the career development approach provides learning opportunities for both the student who plans to continue his education beyond high school, and the student who wishes to enter the job market immediately upon graduation. For example, a student in the medical technology cluster might be planning to go to medical school eventually; another might become a hospital lab technician directly after leaving high school. In either case, his or her experience will provide a marketable skill for making a living or for defraying college expense.

1

An April 1976 federal court order mandated the opening of four centrally located Magnet Schools in the fall of that same year. Because of the success of the Skyline program, the school district was able to organize these schools and recruit the students in a remarkably brief time. Without the already existing curriculum, core teaching staff and students, the opening would have been virtually impossible to achieve by the required date.

The decision was made to use clusters already in effect in Skyline to form the basis for four Magnet Schools: Arts Magnet High School; Business and Management Center; High School for Health Professions; and Transportation Institute. At the beginning of the 1977-78 school year, two additional Magnets were begun—the Human Services Center, and the Law and Public Administration Center. An outstanding professional, rather than an educator, was hired as director of each of these six schools. (For example, the world-renowned Paul Baker, Director of the Dallas Theater Center, was hired as Director of the Arts Magnet.) Administrative functions of the schools were overseen by educators in the position of Assistant Director/Principal.

Critical to the success of the Skyline effort, as well as of the Magnets, has been the intense involvement of the business community. Outstanding professionals in appropriate fields have assisted the school district in a wide variety of ways: they have served on advisory boards, have helped develop the curriculum, and have monitored the programs to assure that the equipment and approaches are kept current with practice in the field. They also serve as resource persons in the classroom, donate materials and equipment, and often provide field trips and training stations for students. For example, students at the High School for Health Professions often observe procedures in Dallas' leading hospitals; they are even allowed to visit intensive care units. These students have advanced study opportunities usually reserved for college-level students. In fact, a lab instructor at the Health Magnet said that she herself did not have the opportunity to perform some of the tests Magnet students are working on in high school until she had graduated from college and was working in a lab.

Optional educational opportunities are also offered Dallas students at the elementary and middle school levels. For example, any Dallas Independent School District student (grades four through six) can apply for entrance to any of the five Vanguard schools. Vanguards include the Mark Twain Fundamental School, the Amelia Earhart Montessori School, the Sidney Lanier Center for Expressive Arts, the Maynard Jackson Center for Individually Guided Education, and the K.B. Polk Center for the Academically Talented and Gifted.

Seventh or eighth graders in the district may apply to attend any of the five academies in the Dallas area. One of these is the Pearl C. Anderson Academy, which focuses on career exploration and allows students to study particular fields of work and make excursions to observe types of occupations in action. A second is the William H. Atwell Academy, which continues the program for academically talented and gifted students available at the Polk Vanguard. A third is the Oliver Wendell Holmes Academy, a classical school emphasizing in-depth study in all areas: e.g., students study foreign languages, learn to write their own computer-assisted instruction programs, and delve into such advanced studies as statistics and oceanography. The fourth is the Sequoyah Environmental Science Academy, which enables students to investigate horticulture, bacteriology, botany, zoology, air and water pollution, and ecology, in addition to their regular studies. Finally, the Alex W. Spence Academy continues the program for the academically talented which is available to younger students at K.B. Polk.

The Magnet School may very well play a starring role in the melodrama of current public education. In fact, it may turn out to be the Number One hero helping to restore the public's confidence in the public schools. One indication of this is the fact that some parents of students who reside within suburban school district boundaries are choosing to pay monthly tuition to send their children to Dallas high school Magnets.

The Magnet School concept, then, can be considered critical to the future of public education in the United States. In order for the public schools to remain viable institutions, educators must offer many different options—options to meet the diverse needs of a modern, ever-changing society and the varying interests of parents and students. The Magnet School approach presents a workable method for developing schools of choice to match exactly the needs and goals of each student.

Magnet Schools also play an increasingly successful role in the desegregation of education institutions. They bring together students of different races and backgrounds who have common interests and goals, but for educational reasons rather than for the simple exercise of mixing bodies. In a Magnet School setting, racial and socio-economic barriers come tumbling down more rapidly than they do in settings where there may be an equal mix of races, but where there may also exist an isolating distance between these races.

The exciting thing is that the Magnet School is a sound approach to education. Parents will choose to send their children to schools where they can find the best and the most positive educational opportunity. Magnet Schools can, and will continue to compete successfully with the finest private schools anywhere.

The Magnet School is the wave of the future, both in terms of its academic excellence, and of the hope it offers youngsters of every race and background. For this reason, I asked Dr. Don Waldrip to coordinate the First Annual International Conference on Magnet Schools in Dallas in March of this year. It was out of that successful conference that the following collection of presentations comes. Our purpose was threefold: to expand our own knowledge by bringing together minds outside, yet involved with, the field of education; to share what we had learned with other educators and interested people; and to move rapidly toward the implementation of a solid educational concept that will serve students well today and will also prepare them for the diverse choices which await them in the twenty-first century.

Nolan Estes, Superintendent
Dallas Independent School District

History and Philosophy of Alternative Schools

1

History and Philosophy of Alternative Schools

MARIO D. FANTINI

Introduction

The main job facing educators today is to convert our universal school system into a universal educational system. So says Mario Fantini in the following keynote address, delivered to the First Annual International Conference on Magnet Schools, Dallas, Texas, on March 9-12, 1977. Dr. Fantini traces the development of educational options through four generations–beginning with the alternatives which were, in fact, outside the public schools, and ending with the present concept of Magnet Schools and the use of community resources. He believes that, prior to the advent of alternatives, quality education (which focused on basic skill development) was possible only for those who fit into the system. Now, however, it focuses both on talent and on basic skill development, and educational systems are asked to develop programs that will reflect the diversity of the students they serve.

America's public schools are now experiencing the beginning of an important reform movement (commonly referred to as "alternatives" or "options") based on student, parent, and teacher choice. This development promises to achieve what previous efforts have not, yet to do so without falling victim to faddism, and without relinquishing the best of what we now have or alienating professionals and laypersons associated with existing school patterns.

A Gallup Poll conducted in 1973 reported that sixty-two percent of parents and eighty percent of professional educators felt that providing options for students was a good idea. This was before the notion of alternatives was well-known. In fact, prior to 1970, there was little in the literature that specifically addressed itself to alternative public schools. In contrast, in 1976 the National School Boards Association's Research Report indicated that "...one quarter of the school board members have alternative schools functioning in their school districts currently."

It is our conviction that the alternative school trend is part of a larger movement affecting the entire definition and structure of American public education, since such options and choices are a crucial initial stage of a multi-phased updating of the public school system of the United States. Briefly, the direction this transformation is taking is as follows: we have created a universal public *school* system, but what our advanced technical society now needs is a universal public *educational* system. Converting a *school* system to an *educational* system will be the aim of the major policy directives in the future.

Clearly, the stakes are high and, unless alternative schools are successful, we may place in danger the entire future of American public education. However, we are getting somewhat ahead of our account. Perhaps it makes sense for us to review how this trend toward alternatives to public schools first arose, our experience with first and second generation attempts at developing optional learning environments, and, finally, what lessons have been learned from these experiences.

Alternatives to Public Schools: First Generation

The first alternatives to public schools were *outside* the public school system. In one sense, all private schools fit this category. After all, if one was affluent enough or, for that matter, felt strongly enough about a particular kind of school (say, a spiritually-oriented school), there were many private schools from which to choose. Similarly, prep schools, academies, Montessori schools, etc., were available to those who had the money to pay the tuition.

Though the alternative schools created in the 1960's were also private schools, they clearly surfaced as reactions to the constraints of the public school system, rather than because of economic conditions. This was for good reason. The public schools, in trying to deal with the masses, in trying to respond to societal demands for bringing diverse subcultures into the mainstream of American life, in trying to establish equality, provided instead a standardized structure. This standardized structure has indeed accomplished a great deal but, in recent history, it has begun to experience the strain created by the universal demands for quality education.

During the 1960's, alternative schools responded to the growing aspirations of countercultures or different life-style groups. For the greater part, these schools were freer in form and substance than the public schools. They borrowed heavily from the writings of A.S. Neill and his Summerhill model, as well as from the so-called romantic public school critics of that period: Goodman, Holt, Kohl, Kozol, Dennison, Herndon, etc.

At first, there were very few branches of the free schools. One branch promoted the "freedom works" philosophy of A.S. Neill; another interpreted "freedom" as liberation of the oppressed. In the former case, free schools were settings in which the learner was in complete charge of his or her own learning: i.e., what is learned, when, where, why, how, and with whom. In the latter group of freedom schools, on the other hand, the important lessons had to do with liberation struggle, the evils of a capitalist economy and political system, and the like.

Allen Graubard studied these alternatives to the public school and indicated that they would be declining significantly in number by the early 1970's.[1] Briefly, the reason he gave for this was limited resources, i.e., money problems. A handful of dedicated teachers working round-the-clock for substandard wages were trying to run a school on a shoestring. Nonetheless, they did serve to inform the public schools that other ways of educating learners were possible.

The civil rights movement of the 1960's also contributed to the promotion of alternative schools. There were occasions, for example, in which school boycotts in protest to segregation resulted in the establishment of temporary alternative school settings in church basements. These were staffed by community persons who developed formats different from those of the public schools. These community schools still dealt with the three "R's," but they also included the history of Black people, what the civil rights movement was all about, and how schools could be tied to community needs.

Some of these schools led to more permanent structures during the late 60's and early 70's — e.g., street academies associated with the Urban League. Harlem Prep also developed as an alternative school — first, outside the public schools and funded by foundations, business, and industry; later, as one of New York City's public schools. Still other independent private schools became places which catered to "disruptive" students, often with public school support in the form of tuition payments.

A third development which served to promote alternatives was the so-called "open classroom" phase that emerged during the late 60's and early 70's. There was a flurry of interest in the United States in the British experience with "informal classrooms and integrated day." Silberman's *Crisis in the Classroom,* a widely-read book of the time, further served to highlight these types of classrooms.

The result of all these trends was to bring to the attention of concerned citizens and professionals the need for more variety in education, especially in *public* education. In this sense, the development of alternative private schools played an important role in bringing the concept of options to the public sector.

At about this same time, another proposal was given widespread attention — educational vouchers. Linked to such prominent economists as Milton Friedman, the idea was to consider education as a free marketplace with the learners and families as consumers, a market which would provide each family with a voucher that could be redeemed at a school of choice. Having families shop around for the kind of school that best satisfied their taste would result in increased options. The proponents of this idea also felt that this method of school finance would assist in equalizing opportunities for the poor.

With federal government support, a number of planning grants were made to the public schools. Many of these planning efforts became highly controversial, generating much criticism from professional educators; others went beyond the planning stage to implementation — the most notable being Alum Rock, California, which is in full operation at the present time.

Options Within the Public Schools:
First and Second Generations

The public schools began to consider options about 1970. The first generation alternatives introduced were primarily adaptations of "free schools" *within* "the system." These were generally subschools separate from the main school, and with more fluid settings. The teachers and students attracted to these alternative schools were usually middle-class whites who were perceived to be "bright and intellectual," but who had rejected the more formal and conventional structure of the public schools. Their non-traditional appearance triggered a mainstream label of "hippie" for the kinds of schools they attended. Such perceptions and labels contributed to a negative image of early alternative schools.

Another branch of first generation alternatives involved separate schools for dropouts, unwed mothers, disruptives, etc. These were perceived as "dumping grounds" for the problem students in public schools. Again, the general perception of alternatives was somehow related to special problem students — either "turned off" or non-academic. In short, they were viewed as special places for other than the "straight type" learner who belonged in the "regular" school.

Still a third major sector of first generation alternatives focused on urban school districts. As a result of the massive performance failures of poor children, new patterns of schooling surfaced. The Parkway Project in Philadelphia, for example, moved away from the schoolhouse and claimed the entire city and its resources as "the school." This school-without-walls attracted a diverse student population, thus promoting integration of different socioeconomic and racial groups.

Berkeley, California, became one of the first city districts to embark on a full-scale alternative schools program. With the assistance of foundations and federal funds, the Berkeley public schools mounted over twenty school options in elementary and secondary schools. These included basic skills centers, multi-cultural school settings, commercially-based learning, environmentally-oriented programs, independent contract curriculum, and the like.[2]

New York City's Haaren High School, the site of the motion picture, *Up The Down Staircase,* embarked on a mini-school concept, with the assistance of the Urban Coalition, that broke a big high school into smaller units with more personalized relationships.

In Cincinnati, a major effort at alternatives resulted in a wide range of options including Montessori education which had previously been restricted to private schools.

Minneapolis mounted an alternative experiment in the southeast section of that city. With the assistance of federal monies, four different kinds of schools were formed: *contemporary,* a traditional approach; *open,* based on informal classroom design; *continuous progress,* based on an ungraded format; and *free,* where the individual directs his or her own learning. The experience with this project led to a system-wide policy promoting alternatives.

Philadelphia also formed an Office of Alternative Education to oversee the more than fifty alternatives developed in its city schools.

Taken together, these first generation options served to introduce the notion of alternatives to the public schools. The fact that they were perceived to focus for the most part on the "special" cases had a double effect. On the one hand, the public schools were eager to find some solution to the nagging problems which faced them. Trying to get a response from those middle-class students who were "turned off," from those who were about to drop out, from those who were acting out deeper frustrations, as well as from those who were not achieving academically for other reasons represented a continuing concern of the public schools — a concern that could perhaps be best dealt with through alternative schools.

On the other hand, establishing possible solutions to these problems through alternatives served to reeducate the mainstream and introduce it to what the idea behind alternatives was all about. The reasoning of this mainstream often was that, since alternatives seemed to have something to do with the *problem* kids in the schools, they could have little to do with the *other* students. In fact, if alternatives were proposed for regular students, the question might arise — why? After all there is nothing wrong with a regular student; he or she is normal. And alternatives were only for those who were not really normal!

The seeds for the second generation alternatives were also sown during this same period. A new crop of options emerged between 1972 and 1976 that moved into the mainstream schools — middle-class by nature and located in the affluent areas of the suburbs. The surfacing of such options represented an important development since, in political terms, the mainstream plays a gatekeeper role in the American public school system. That is to say, any major reform has to be acceptable to that mainstream if it is to become a serious public school undertaking. If it is not acceptable, the mainstream can veto most proposals for altering the public schools. On the other hand, if the mainstream accepts a proposal, this can make all the difference. As a matter of fact, we are now at a point at which it appears that alternatives have begun to win such approval, and this support has been a direct outgrowth of our experience with second generation options.

For example, in Brookline, Massachusetts, a wealthy suburb of Boston, the high school there was organized to offer over a dozen options in an attempt to update the concept of the "comprehensive" high school.

For its part, Quincy II High School in Quincy, Illinois, a typical middle-American community, undertook a process of cooperative planning involving parents, teachers, and students that resulted in a school-within-a-school arrangement. This Quincy Education by Choice model won national acclaim. Originally a high school for 1,500 students and 80 teachers, it became five subschools, each offering a distinctive type of program. These included traditional, flexible, individual, fine arts, and career schools.

Finally, in Pasadena, California, two alternatives — one, an open high school; the other, a fundamental school emphasizing a return to basics and to more traditional values — brought the idea of a range of options into sharper focus.

In many of America's suburbs and rural schools, options began to emerge — whether these were in the form of semester options, classroom options, or schools-within-schools. They were introduced, usually, through cooperative planning that involved administration, teachers, parents, and students.

Options spread next to the state level. Illinois and New York created offices for alternative schools, while in California, an alternative school assembly bill was passed.[3] These developments and many others began to point to the emergence of alternatives as a serious reform effort in American education. Some higher education institutions were likewise involved. Indiana University developed a Center for Options in Public Education, and the University of Massachusetts/Amherst, its Center for Alternative Schools. The Indiana Group also helped form the International Consortium for Options in Public Education.

LESSONS LEARNED

During both the first and second generation alternatives, there were important lessons learned. One lesson had to do with the need for retaining the *traditional* in these alternatives. Certain options, for example, projected the idea that they were superior to traditional forms by implying that conventional schools were "bad" in comparison. This only served to alienate most of those connected with traditional schools — usually, the majority of the teachers, parents, and administrators of the community.

It should be remembered that traditional schools as the normative pattern have attempted to respond to the accelerating needs of a changing society, but have ended up instead by being overloaded. We have expected traditional schools, unfairly perhaps, to do what no other pattern of schooling has done — to reach everyone. If we could replace traditional with, say, Montessori schools and yet require everyone to attend, we would end up by also overloading Montessori schools and then criticizing them for not doing the job, either. The facts appear to justify the conclusion that, if no one model works for everyone, then perhaps a variety of models, made available by choice, could relieve the strain on any one pattern and, at the same time perhaps, reach more learners.

A second lesson concerns the use and misuse of labels. Eager at times to have the caption of a program reveal the style of that program, those associated with it would use such descriptive labels as "open" or "humanistic." These and other similar labels, if not carefully developed, could have a negative consequence. To begin with, if an option is labeled "open," it implies the others are somehow "closed." Similarly those who are not associated with humanistic options may exclaim, "Does this mean that we are dehumanistic?" If they come to feel this, they may become defensive, and the spirit of cooperation, essential in district-wide or school-wide planning, will as a consequence be jeopardized.

Allied to these two lessons is a third: namely, that for options to flourish, they need a strong public and professional base of understanding and support. The philosophy of options must make sense to the major interested parties and must be perceived by them as furthering the goals of their school district. Planning must be set up in such a way that *all* parties connect; in short, if the school district is to embark on options, then it must do so with the full understanding of all. In the same way, if the district gives options a priority, then it must do this with everyone's understanding and backing. Too often, unfortunately, options spring up as isolated pieces without any real connection to the ongoing programs. Clearly, this implies a lack of contact with the larger community, especially with parents and other taxpayers.

ALTERNATIVE GUIDELINES

The lessons identified above can serve as *guidelines* for public school districts participating in alternative schools. These guidelines include the following principles:

1. Alternatives are not superimposed, but are a matter of choice for all participants — teachers, parents, and students.
2. Alternatives should be viewed as another legitimate way of providing education *alongside* the existing pattern. At the same time, they are different from special programs for dropouts, unwed mothers, and the like.
3. Alternative schools do not practice exclusivity.
4. They do not make exaggerated claims of accomplishments that could be deceptive in the long run.
5. They are aimed at a broad, common set of *educational* objectives, not just limited objectives. Alternative public schools are responsible to the public for comprehensive, cognitive, and affective goals that cannot be compromised. These goals include such things as basic skills, learning how to learn, talent development, socialization of basic societal roles (citizen, consumer, worker), and self-concept development.
6. Alternative schools do not cost more money than existing per student expenditures in the public schools.
7. These programs are evaluated. [4]

We can now specify more clearly the entire spectrum of optional learning environments based on individualized styles of learning. The earlier fuzziness about the instructional process has given way to sharper delineation. For instance, alternatives are now being considered along a continuum of the factors involved in the utilization of educational resources — by whom are they used, for whom, when, where, how, and why. By focusing on this type of *resource orchestration*, we can come up with a broadened conception of alternatives, such as the one indicated below:

A.	*B.*
Individual learner decides what he or she learns – when, where, why, and with whom.	*Institution decides for the learner what is learned – where, when, why, and with whom.*

At one end of the spectrum, the individual learner, no matter what his age, orchestrates his own education by deciding what to learn, when, where, how, why, and with whom. At the other end, an institution, usually the school, makes all these decisions for him. In the first case (A), an individual learner may decide to study Chinese at Berlitz, learn writing from a journalist, listen to the world's great music at a free library, take guided tours of art and science museums, travel to different countries, assume an apprenticeship in a law office, etc. At this level, the learner uses and tailors these already existing educational resources to fit his own needs and style. For example, he may prefer to arrange his activities for the late afternoon and evening (rather than have the time and place imposed) because he thinks of himself as a "night person" whose "body time" is geared to the evening. Another learner may be a morning person, etc. In any event, under the individual educational orchestration, guidance is available upon request. The learner is a consumer of various educational services which are purchased as needed: e.g., tutors, seminars, tours.

In the second case (B), society delegates to an *institution*, most often a school, the responsibility for orchestrating the resources that can educate the greatest number of persons. Schools select such resources as buildings, certified teachers, books, audio-visual equipment, desks, etc. The institution then certifies to the society that each learner has achieved a minimum level of competence (*e.g.*, high school diploma). Certain institutions prescribe uniformly for all learners; others are more flexible.

As the search for knowledge in a number of fields like health, science, government, and art expands and becomes more complex, only *experts* in these areas can help us acquire the competencies we need. For example, as our nutritional needs become increasingly complex, we must seek guidance from the experts. Clearly it is difficult for school teachers to be knowledgeable in all these areas. Some educators are therefore suggesting that agencies such as hospitals, medical schools, and pharmaceutical houses make their resources available to schools for education in the health fields.[5]

Magnet School Alternatives: Third and Fourth Generations

In addition to offering variety in the curriculum, the concept of alternatives has also been used in an attempt to solve the long-standing problem of segregation in schools by promoting desegregation. Since alternative learning environments involve distinctive features that can be attractive to different learners, why not have these environments serve as a "magnet?"

Magnet Schools started in places like Philadelphia in science-rich schools, arts-oriented schools, and the like, and then slowly expanded into such community resources as schools-without-walls. This move from the *magnet as schoolhouse* to the *magnet as a community-based center* was very important. The historical identification of education as something that takes place in a special building and with a certain standardization of conceptions has forced most laymen into associating good (and bad) schools not so much with the quality of the programs they offer as with the socioeconomic composition of their students and the neighborhood in

which they are located. In other words, a good school i
students attend — which usually means middle-class

The pioneering efforts of Dallas and Houston hav(
conception of quality public education. But, in ord
discussion of such third and fourth generation optior
philosophy underlying the Dallas and Houston approac
point.

Alternatives have called attention to differences in programs, rather than in
social class or race. However, since *status* and *prestige* are important contributors
to our perceptions of "good" and "quality," the move toward community-based
options has capitalized on these social values. Art centers, museums, insurance
companies, banks, medical schools, government offices, doctors, lawyers, musi-
cians, sculptors — all have begun to become involved in alternative-oriented
schools.

Thus have the seeds of third and fourth generation alternatives been planted.
If properly nurtured, these seeds can yield fruit which will significantly alter the
form and shape of American public education, and the role of professional
educators as well.

Third and fourth generation options will build on the cumulative wisdom of
the past to form the context of education for the next century. Still, our vision of
converting a school system to an educational system will depend on how well we
deal with these third and fourth generation alternatives.

Thus far, the trend toward increased options for parents, teachers, students,
and administrators has served to legitimize variety within the public school
system. People are now getting comfortable with the idea that there are many roads
both to learning and to quality education. Given our political and economic
diversity, options that emphasize personal choice reduce potential conflict — this
because the threat of imposed formats is largely removed.

Whether one is an educational conservative or liberal, options provide an
acceptable approach. At the same time, this approach supports both the value of
diversity and the need for unity in education. That is to say, we become unified by
our common commitment to diversity as the means for achieving quality education.

Still, a task remains to be addressed: namely, identifying the common
ingredients in quality education. This becomes particularly crucial in an era in
which attaining quality education is no longer a privilege, but a civil right. The
right to quality education for every American is becoming accepted. Yet, guaranteeing each person quality education will necessitate an updated system of public
education — i.e., a public *educational* system.

In order to get us thinking about alternatives and their role in the development
of a modernized system of public education, it may be useful to sketch a definition
of quality education before moving on to new alternatives for increasing the
likelihood that all learners will be fully educated by the beginning of the twenty-
first century.

quality education includes the following set of objectives:

A. *Basic Skills* — reading, writing, arithmetic, and the so-called survival competencies necessary to promote further learning.

B. *Talent-Identification and Cultivation* — the acceptance of the fact that every person can develop a talent and that this talent can lead him to a career which is financially and psychologically rewarding.

C. *Competencies to Perform Mature Adult Roles* — despite the belief that the educated person knows implicitly how to perform these roles (*e.g.*, citizen, consumer, parent, etc.), the realization of such competencies by all citizens should be an explicit goal of the educational process.

D. *Self-Worth* — the belief that, through education, a person learns to feel good about himself.[6]

This set of objectives *cannot be left to chance.* Some societal agency must assume responsibility and accountability for insuring that each citizen has ample opportunities to be educated, and that agency is the public school.

One reason these objectives are so crucial is that they are closely tied to a person's sense of *fate control* — one of the most powerful motivators known. If a person possesses the skills, concepts, and attitudes that promote a sense of control over his own destiny, he is likely to feel good about himself. On the other hand, if a person cannot even read or write, he is more likely to be dependent, more likely to be oppressed. Similarly, a person who has not had an opportunity to develop a talent will feel less fulfilled, less educated.

While people appear to agree on the broad goals of quality education, they differ on the *means* of achieving them. Some families, for example, feel that they would like the school to deal primarily with the basics and that other objectives are really the domain of the home. Certainly, a wealthy family can hire tutors in ballet, languages, music, arts, literature, etc. Wealthy parents are more likely to use travel as a basic mode of education. Poorer families, on the other hand, must rely increasingly on public institutions to deliver such quality education. As we move closer to a policy in which quality education is a *right,* rather than a privilege, then the need to guarantee *each* learner access to such an education will result in a greater delegation of authority to educational institutions.[7]

In most discussions of alternative education, we have often neglected the real strengths of the communities and the rich resources that are concentrated there — resources that can be tapped to enhance learning for the next generation. Cities, especially, are rich centers: the medical, legal, and arts communities prosper here; business and industry flourish; the communications industry is prominent. Museums, libraries, and other scientific and cultural units are also located in these urban settings. These are resources that are difficult to duplicate in suburban areas, and are the very resources that can be tapped and utilized to form our new educational environments. These are the resources which, over time, have achieved status in the eyes of the general public. There is little question that most Americans believe medical complexes are places inhabited by very competent people, that performing arts centers are the places which cater to the most gifted artists, that radio and television are places in which the experts in communications are employed, that newspaper offices are places in which some of the finest writers are housed, etc. And these are the very resources which magnet school alternatives have begun to tap.

Magnet Schools

Magnet School alternatives have begun to show the public that they can become educational settings in which students can live and learn. The idea of using community resources to improve learning is not new, of course. Most school systems engage in community visits through field trips. Similarly, many schools invite experts from the community into the school. In some cases, too, the schools have cooperative relationships with business and industry through such programs as junior achievement and cooperatives. However, until recently we have not taken the bigger step of moving education directly into these real-world environments as a logical expansion of the classroom. The focus on the four walls of the school as the major legitimate boundary in which learning takes place has conditioned most of our thinking about education. In fact, keeping students in school has often been synonymous with improved learning. Similarly, building modern schools has been viewed as important because they were the places in which such improved learning took place. In any event, the focus has invariably been on the *schoolhouse*. But, as was pointed out earlier, this model has led to serious drawbacks because the schoolhouse was and is unable to deal effectively with human *diversity*.

There is a different concept of quality education, though. What if a *new school* were planned, located on the premises of a prominent institution in the community? What if noted artists were to work with public school officials on a new Fine Arts Learning Center located in a city's performing arts complex? What if one were to conceptualize a Metropolitan Opera High School or San Francisco Opera High School or a Modern and Classical Dance High School or a Bell Laboratories Science Center High School or a University of Pennsylvania Business High School? What if we conceived a situation in which a series of alternative "schools" were created, based *not* on the social class composition of students but on the *quality* of the program being offered? For instance, what if we had a high school for the medical arts located in a famous medical complex? What if doctors, nutritionists, and researchers became part of a new faculty interested in working with those students who had identified the pursuit of medical careers as a major area of interest? Certainly, such a "school" would have status in the eyes of students and parents — whether they were from urban or suburban areas. The facilities would naturally be modern since they would be utilized to prepare the next generation of doctors, and would also include the latest in technology and library facilities. Since such medical complexes are usually part of a university system, with a little more planning graduate and undergraduate college students could be included in the program so that every high school student enrolling in a medical arts high school could have an individual *tutor* in any field: e.g., basic reading, writing, literature, math, etc. That is to say, college students as part of their course work could engage in tutorial work.

Or consider a high school for languages or international studies. Perhaps these high school students are interested in working in other countries. Well then, they would be placed in a learning context which would equip them with those attitudes and skills necessary for fulfilling their career responsibilities. This, in fact, is just what has been pioneered by the Public School Systems of Houston, Chicago, and Boston.

Consider, too, cities located near large bodies of water. One could conceive of having a high school there for oceanography and navigation. Similarly, in the proper surroundings, one could have a high school for aviation or space technology, while our governmental centers could become alternative schools for law and government.[8]

Finally, insurance firms could make resources available for driver education; business and industry, for careers; cultural agencies, for the aesthetic aspirations, etc. Again, the students would be *attracted* to the Magnet alternative, and integration would be achieved as a normal consequence.

No matter how resource utilization is conceptualized, the idea of alternatives is crucial and is certainly a central theme in the debate now brewing over the future course of American education.[9]

As previously indicated, we are already planting the seeds for such an educational system. In Dallas, for example, the following Magnet alternatives are in motion:

TRANSPORTATION INSTITUTE. Will be located in a former automotive facility at 2200 Ross Avenue, and will include a new-car showroom, a repair center with the latest equipment, and a complete auto rebuilding facility.

"It will be," said Rodger Meier, "a comprehensive classroom laboratory and on-the-job training program designed for students who are interested in the sale and marketing, mechanics and service, or rebuilding of motor vehicles, and will permit them to specialize in the field of their choice."

BUSINESS AND MANAGEMENT CENTER. Located in the central business district, will train young men and women in all phases of business and management. The program will begin with a thorough orientation to the basics of the business world, taught by skilled instructors and working professionals. Basic subjects will include accounting, data entry and processing, concepts of American business, typing and shorthand (including machine shorthand).

Students will then select areas for specialization, according to Lee Turner, "including advanced accounting, banking, investments, insurance, real estate, data processing, and secretarial science. This specialized program includes advanced skill development and instruction, but emphasizes in-the-field employment with pay while students are still in school to give each student professional experience and supervision."

CREATIVE ARTS ACADEMY. Offers the facilities, artists, and instruction to develop student interest and talent in two basic areas — the performing arts and the visual arts. Set amid the cultural atmosphere of Dallas' museums and theaters, and drawing on the total artistic and educational resources of the area, this curriculum offers students the intensive instruction they require to prepare for a professional career.

"We are tremendously excited by the potential for the Creative Arts Academy in Dallas," said John D. Murchison, "and are particularly pleased by the possibility of having Paul Baker, one of the nation's foremost theater directors, direct this curriculum. We cannot imagine a finer opportunity for Dallas youth to train and learn in the field of creative arts."

The performing arts curriculum will be divided into three areas: music, dance, and theater arts. Students will be educated in the fundamentals, then will move into individual and group performance. The third phase will include elective study in specific areas for future training.

Visual arts will begin with a thorough exposure to all visual forms, including two- and three-dimensional art and applied design. Students will be instructed in the twelve basic concepts common to the visual arts, and then will be afforded an opportunity to apply those concepts to drawing, painting, printmaking, metal, wood and stone sculpture, ceramics, weaving, stitchery, macrame, and jewelry design. An academy gallery will enable students to exhibit and sell their works to the public.

HEALTH PROFESSIONALS CURRICULUM. Will offer the necessary training to equip graduates for immediate positions as nurses' aides, and dental and medical lab and office assistants. The center also will offer excellent preparation for students interested in attending medical or dental school eventually or in entering other advanced health professions.

Initially, each student is taught all-purpose skills that can be applied to numerous career positions. From there, the students will begin intensive instruction in medical or dental technology.

"With the critical shortage of medical and dental support personnel, thousands of positions are open today requiring trained professionals at all skill levels," pointed out Boone Powell.

The medical careers program will include a thorough course in basic anatomy and physiology taught by a registered M.D. This course will prepare the way for more intensive study in medical laboratory work, disease analysis, nurse science, physical therapy, and other health-related fields.

Dental technology instruction will prepare the student in such diverse areas as prosthetics, crowns, and bridgework. Paid on-the-job internships in professional laboratories are likewise offered. Also included are dental techniques, and equipment and office management, followed by actual working experience in dental anatomy, lab procedures, and dental assisting skills.

The Health Professions Center will offer its advanced students paid field positions for extensive practical experience.[10]

Let us consider for a moment the World Trade Center in Dallas. By any criteria, this complex is impressive. It has the latest in facilities and equipment, as well as an atmosphere rich in finance, marketing, sales, design, languages, human relations, and the like. In brief, it is a *powerful* educational environment. For this instructionally oriented trade center to prosper, clearly some of the most gifted persons from these fields had to be tapped. Now let us consider this question: Could any public or private high school hope to duplicate the resources of a World Trade Center? Obviously not. However, through imaginative planning, there could be a World Trade High School located in such a center, offering thousands of young persons from all backgrounds an opportunity to learn in a real-world laboratory of unparalleled potential.[11]

The list of possibilities could easily be expanded. But the important point here is that these alternatives are powerful educational environments which in their own right can attract students, not by *force* but by *choice*. Since these will be new optional learning environments, they can be treated as such under the auspices of the public schools. By treating them as new "schools," the public school system can develop brochures announcing their opening and the fact that they will cater to a larger audience: i.e., all students who are interested, whether they attend urban or suburban schools. And since they are *public* schools, they will practice *non-exclusivity,* and will establish as a policy the desirability of a diverse student population, without reference to sex, age, or class. Finally, because the overriding attraction will be the quality of the program, the students will come together by *choice,* a much more natural way of achieving integration than the present attempts to force the issue.

Clinical Findings

On this emotional issue of desegregation, it may be useful to review here certain clinical findings. It appears that the concept of the "Magnet School," which attempts to offer specialized programs as a means of attracting a racially diverse student body, has drawn mixed reviews. Thus, while the idea of emphasizing quality programs at different school sites was seen as a sensible proposal, its direct linkage to desegregation produced a counter effect. While this was understandable, it clearly posed a threat to the Magnet School concept.

How can this threat be dealt with? Well, it should be remembered that alternative education which uses potent community resources in off-school-site settings can best be introduced to the public as an attempt on the part of the public school system to offer expanded opportunities for quality service. When it becomes clear to the public that businessmen, scientists, pilots, writers, and poets, as well as the institutions they're associated with are closely connected to alternative education and so guarantee quality, then its initial image for the educational consumer will be more sharply and positively delineated. Certainly, a High School for Finance located on Wall Street, or a Center for Oceanography located at the University of Miami (each of them servicing an integrated student body), would not find difficulty in gaining consumer approval. Again, the emphasis here would be on the quality of the program, rather than on deliberate attempts to achieve racial balance. And, since quality education is the common goal for all groups, its emphasis would be generally welcome.

As a way, perhaps, of launching a number of alternative learning centers, the assistance of prominent figures from each talent field could be enlisted (a Helen Hayes in dramatic arts, a Sammy Davis Jr. in the entertainment arts, a Leonard Bernstein in musical arts, a prima ballerina in the dance arts, a prominent surgeon in the medical arts, a top financeer in the financial arts, etc.). In each case, such a recognized figure or figures would become associated with the alternative center in much the same way that many of our summer camps advertised in Sunday newspapers indicate that a major sports figure, for example, will be involved in their programs to lend competent guidance.

The overall psychological point being made here is that the public, conditioned by long years of association with the conventional notions of schooling, needs to be reached on terms that will reassure it. To achieve this, they will first of all be contacted as educational *consumers* rather than as clients; that is to say, as parents and students with a *right* to choice, rather than an imposed format. Secondly, the association of the alternative with the public school system which parents and students are already familiar with will further help in the task of reassurance. Thirdly, the connection of clearly established and recognizable leaders in talent fields with the alternative school will lend it a legitimizing, qualitative dimension.

If the cornerstone of the conventional schoolhouse is the *3 R's,* then the cornerstone of this new alternative school is *talent*. Historically, the public school model was initiated within the context of a predominantly rural economy. This meant that at a time when most Americans worked on the farm, their career and vocational aspirations were inevitably much more limited. In such a setting, sending their children to school basically meant learning the 3 R's — reading, especially.

Much of our present school structure is still rooted in that agrarian culture. In fact, the retention of the "summer vacation" is symbolic of this — summer being the time when the young were expected on the farm for the harvest. Further, the "add-ons" that have been made in an attempt to update the schools (e.g., vocational education) have resulted for the most part in tracking systems and the like. Clearly, these add-ons by themselves cannot now carry us into the twenty-first century.

By emphasizing *talent,* it does not mean the new system of public education will neglect other educational objectives, including basics. On the contrary, these will be equally emphasized but, unlike the case in the past, the mode of teaching these skills will be geared to each learner's quest for developing a talent. Having cultivated a talent, that person can more readily achieve inner fulfillment, and increase his sense of fate control and sense of self-esteem. Conversely, not having had the opportunity to cultivate a talent can leave a person vulnerable, underdeveloped, and dependent on seeking a job for survival reasons alone. The talented person who appropriately uses his or her talent in the marketplace has a far greater chance of attaining career gratification — fiscal *and* psychic — than a person who has not had this chance.

Moreover, *talent* rivals the 3 R's in terms of status and prestige. (Once again, the public image is important here.) Taken together, talent and the 3 R's can create a potent image of quality education, one that is clearly associated with the new system of public education.

However, it should be emphasized here that few, if any, of these talent-centered, community-based alternatives can be mounted *without careful planning*. And this takes *time* and *leadership*. Again, public schools, chief school officers, and school boards are in key positions of influence. They can trigger the planning process. The time dimension is of course equally important. In the past, it has sometimes been assumed that, after conceptualizing a proposal, to implement the process is a rather simple matter. Obviously, though, this is far from being the case. The complexities of planning and implementation are well known by anyone who has ever attempted to deal with change. Further, the tendency to promise a great deal at the start (i.e., when announcing a new program) is tempting. Yet we all know that building unrealistic expectations can lead to frustration and further disillusionment.

If sound foundations for new alternative public schools are not established, they will not possess the capability of delivering what was promised. This can have a devastating effect on how alternatives will be perceived by the majority of citizens, and thereby limit anew the opportunity they afford of bringing about natural integration.[12]

Such a result would be most unfortunate. For what family would not want its son or daughter to be developing a talent in a setting which has such recognized expertise and civic prestige? Even more to the point, how many parents could afford to send their children to a school that would offer the same opportunities? The Magnet School represents a complex in which youngsters can learn multiple languages, for example, using them in daily conversations with customers from different countries. Still other learners could assume roles in marketing, art, and design methods, or else participate in sales management efforts, etc. Each field would be taught by those with proven skills. The public school would supervise the entire activity through professional educators who would monitor the curriculum for each "high school" student. At the same time, the other general academic subjects could be taught, on the premises, by members of the professional teaching staff who would have access to seminar rooms, media equipment, and the like. Obviously, the qualitative aspects of such a program would be its dominant force. These same qualitative features would be emphasized in making such a learning environment known and acceptable to parents, students, and teachers. Waiting lists of applicants could reasonably be anticipated. And, since a Magnet is a "public school," non-exclusivity would be practiced in its selection process. Therefore, a diverse student body would be the likely result, and racial and class *diversity* would accrue more *naturally*.[13] In fact, over time, a concept similar to that proposed by New York City's Learning Cooperative would begin to emerge

The old and new systems can be presented as follows:*

THE 'NEW' SCHOOL

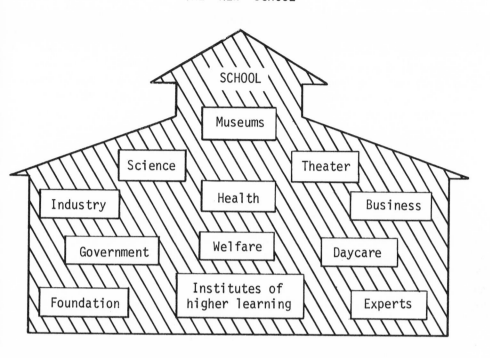

THE 'OLD' SCHOOL

*Adapted from Design for Change, Staff Bulletin, The Public Schools of New York City, May 15, 1972.

— namely, one in which a school system becomes an educational system. (See diagram on page 23.)

After an initial period of cooperative planning with the public schools, the community agencies could then consider "writing off" such services. Certainly, the American Bar Association, American Medical Association, American Manufacturers Association, could make such public service commitments as could Bell Telephone, Prudential Insurance, and First National City Bank. Most of these business and industrial institutions already have public service budget items that could readily be used for such educational purposes.[14]

Conclusion

As America approaches the twenty-first century, there is clearly a new need for quality education. In order for persons to grow and develop in response to new societal demands, quality education is a major requirement.

We have known for some time that education is basic to human and societal development. But now this basic need is being expressed in terms of a universal demand for quality education. In fact, quality education is now seen as a civil *right;* that is to say, it is the right of every American to receive a first-rate education. However, the public school system, as it is presently structured, no longer has the capacity to respond to this demand. The present system of public schooling was designed for an earlier time; yet, societal demands continue to pressure it and those connected with it. The result has been an increase in political activism, with power positions forming among interested parents, teachers, students, administrators, school boards, lay taxpayers, and the like. This period of increased political activity is symptomatic of a broader issue — the updating of our educational institutions.

It is at this stage that alternatives enter the picture. The value our country places on education cannot be compromised by a misreading of the symptoms afflicting our schools. We say that diversity is a belief basic to way of life; we say that people are entitled to their point of view, whether it be conservative or liberal; we say that each person is entitled to a choice. Yet these same principles are not applied to our current public school systems. Instead, we have been looking for *the one way* to do things that will please everyone. But putting all of our eggs in one basket has not been a good practice. By forcing all learners and their families to adjust to a single school model, we have placed a severe strain on both. The normative school has simply not prepared itself for the enormous human diversity that now confronts it, with the result that increasing numbers of learners cannot connect with the scholastic diet being served there. This has caused growing frustration on all sides, and has led to disconnection, discontent, and confrontation.

Moreover, changes in models of schooling have too often represented just that — a switch from one orthodoxy to another, often without considering parent, student, or teacher choice. At times, even, tugs-of-war have been initiated with

groups vying to dominate one another. School board members h
"push" for one form of schooling: *e.g.,* fundamental *or* ope
"four to three" school board majorities have established polic
schools in one direction or another. Obviously, though, mandat
a diverse community is bound to elicit controversy and cause

It is this kind of inflexibility, as well as unresponsiveness to
the educational consumers, that has led to the alternative school movement.
Whether one is an educational conservative or liberal, one still has the right to a
legitimate form of education that is compatible with one's needs. The safety valves
of the past — moving to another community, sending children to private schools,
dropping out of school — are increasingly no longer options. Certainly, "dropping
out" can only result in frustration and dependence. Options within our schools are
therefore an important development which, if properly nurtured, can help update
our current public school system. In fact, options become the vehicle for converting our school system to an *educational* system in which each learner will have
access to quality education as *a matter of right.*

Educationally, alternatives have sought justification in their philosophy of
individualization and personalized learning. There is wide agreement that people
learn in different ways, have different styles, and that there is a range of legitimate,
existing options from which to choose — ungraded, self-contained interdiscipli-
nary, open, fundamental, bilingual, Montessori, work-study, performing arts,
career, community-based, and the like. These optional learning styles can eventually result in the creation of smaller educational units. (The standard school has
been seen by many as being too big, too bureaucratic, and one in which the
individual tends to get lost). Yet, though alternatives help break down the bureaucratic standardization of schools, they do not scrap the virtues of those existing
schools.

Economically, alternatives have gained support because, even though they
are based on a different utilization of *available resources,* they involve the same
per student cost as does the standard school operation. This is particularly the case
with those options *within* the public schools. Those that started as *alternatives* to
the public schools, on the other hand, were based on tuition or on outside fiscal
support.

Politically, the idea of offering options within the framework of the public
education system guarantees that parents and students can choose the educational
setting most desirable to them (*i.e.,* a setting involving a minimum of imposed
formats and an optimum degree of *choice).* In short, professional educators make
sure that each learner, regardless of the setting, has opportunities to achieve *all* of
the objectives that go into a comprehensive concept of quality education. Similarly, options provide an opportunity for a wide spectrum of people with different
personal tastes and styles (the backbone of our pluralistic society) to seek constructive expression. In the increasingly political context in which our school system
finds itself, options can thus offer some hope of pulling us together, rather than of
driving us apart.

Obviously, there are other "spin off" values to cooperative efforts between hool and community. Such joint efforts can build a greater base of understanding and support for the public school system and can lead to a more effective use of available resources, thus minimizing duplication both within and outside the school. Coming as it does at a time when economic constraints face all parties, this result is likely to be welcomed.

Finally, there is something legitimate about the creation of a full or partial school that emphasizes the humanities, performing arts, visual arts, ecology, languages, aerospace, etc., and a school that is located in community settings noted for such orientations. Under such a concept, art museums, libraries, symphony halls, and environmental camps would become learning laboratories, and would offer the attraction of such experts as poets, doctors, scientists, ballerinas, artists, writers, nutritionists, engineers, and the like.

Educational leaders are now in a position to consider the rich resources of the city in terms of reforming the public education system. This can be accomplished without seriously affecting the economic, political, or educational underpinnings of that system. Rather than look at the negative side of urban schools, why not find a way to emphasize the positive aspects of city life? Unfortunately, the process, which seems deceptively simple, will require considerable planning. There are proposals, however, which have recently been put forward that aim at a move in this direction. The RISE Commission Report in California, and the Kettering Report on the Reform of Secondary Schools are but two examples of this. And certainly meetings such as this one offer responsible leaders the opportunity to consider further moves in such a direction.[15]

Legislative Implications of Magnet Schools

2

Legislative Implications of Magnet Schools

SENATOR JOHN GLENN

Introduction

Senator John Glenn of Ohio is committed to the concept of Magnet Schools. In the following paper, he explains in some detail the work he has done in Washington, D.C. that has led to the financing of that commitment. Since Senator Glenn's presentation to the conference in Dallas, his congressional bill, the School Innovation Integration Act, *enacted the fall of 1976 as PL-94-482, has been funded for the Fiscal Year 1977 and 1978.*

When one addresses the subject of Magnet Schools in our society—schools that draw from a broad population, and which attempt to remedy an enormous range of educational, social, familial, and governmental ills—one is addressing, basically, the subject of the incredible interrelatedness of our society. Changing one element here has an effect there — perhaps in an unexpected way. Even in more conservative terms, keeping the *status quo* in one area causes repercussions in another. Our personal lives and the lives of our institutions are so interwoven, in fact, that it is virtually impossible to make a change in one part without affecting the whole. Yet none of us is big enough, bright enough, strong, powerful, or brave enough to tackle the whole with all its ramifications. So we work a little at a time, making small improvements here, and putting out fires on the other end that may result.

Given all the diverse elements in our country, we have developed such a complex, interrelated society that we exist in a kind of modern-day, colonial village where each part pulls its own weight, operating for the good of itself as well as for the good of the whole. If one part breaks down, the other parts suffer. In the old colonial village, there was the cobbler down the street here, the buggy-maker over there, while the vegetables were grown behind the house in yet another place. Consequently, one needed very little from outside that colonial village. But, today, that village concept has expanded so greatly that the garden is in central California, the buggy-maker is in Detroit, and the cobbler probably is not even in this country; he is probably in Italy or another remote place: for today we import about fifty percent of our shoes.

Our expanded interrelatedness can be epitomized by the events of a few years ago, in which the drawbridge operators in New York went on strike. Since there were only about 800 drawbridge operators in New York, everyone thought, so what? It's a joke! Who cares if a few guys want to go on strike? It was a joke—that is, until a few days after the strike was in effect. Then the people on Wall Street were not getting to work; they were running a reduced ship, and, to make a long story short, the entire economic system of our country and of much of the free world was beginning to grind slowly to a halt, simply because of that strike. The 800 drawbridge operators of New York bringing the economic free world to its knees? How much more interrelated can we get?

Similarly, when we talk about Magnet Schools today—seemingly a minute area of our society to focus upon—we are talking about that modern-day colonial village. You all know this just as well, or probably better, than I do. When I look at the very challenging program you have laid out for the next few days of this symposium, I feel a bit like a kid from the farm club during spring training trying to teach big leaguers how to bat. You have been working out in the field on these problems, and I have done a little bit in Washington, but I still think you are far more familiar with many of the details and problems than I. Even the laymen in our urban centers have some appreciation of the significance of Magnet Schools and a basic knowledge of how they function.

I would like to take a few minutes here to discuss my bit of business in Washington that has, I think, complemented your field work in this area. I am referring to the School Integration Innovation Act, and the legislation I introduced in the 94th Congress which stands today as the only federal law that authorizes U.S. money for Magnet Schools—in cases where the schools become part of a desegregation plan.

First, here are some of the underlying assumptions and attitudes that went into my drafting of #S-3319, as the bill was numbered. The goal, as I saw it from the beginning, was to provide schools with superior education—education so attractive to all racial groups that integration would occur naturally, rather than as a result of a governmental requirement. Although I think that some federal judges have moved almost instinctively toward mandatory transportation, I did not offer the bill as a means of short-circuiting court-ordered busing. There are, I believe, some intransigent school systems left in our country which, unfortunately, will not budge from thoroughly segregatory patterns that should have been corrected years ago. I have felt all along that, if the courts as a last resort need busing as a tool—although we hope not the *only* tool—then we will just have to keep this remedy available.

But there should be other options, a variety of different methods available. And to this end I have made efforts to help provide for and to encourage other options and remedies. Having said that, I must say, too, that I still believe the turmoil surrounding this emotional issue has been negative and counterproductive, playing in disheartening fashion upon the legitimate and very understandable concerns of parents.

I introduced the School Integration Innovation Act last April, almost a year ago. At the same time a companion bill in the House was sponsored by two other Ohioans, John Seiberling from Akron, and Charles Whalen of Dayton, one a Democrat and one a Republican; so we had bipartisan support. One of the principal architects of this bill, a man present with me today, was Reg Gilliam, from my staff. Reg is an educator, a former professor and dean at Williams College. He is also an attorney and is from the Harlem area of New York City. He is an outstanding expert on the subject we are addressing.

When we began work on this bill, we thought we needed about one billion dollars to start the program. So, in the bill, we called for an expenditure of one billion dollars a year for the *Emergency School Aid Act* with newly authorized activities that would include:

1. Construction and operation of Magnet Schools. (Now, obviously, when we put the word "construction" in there, the cost went up. We did not get the construction money, and so the cost was scaled down considerably. However, originally that was our number one objective.)

2. Pairing specific schools and programs with specific colleges, universities, and leading businesses in the cities.

3. Development of plans for construction of neutral site schools.

4. Construction and development of education parks.

5. Education programs, specifically designed to improve the quality of inner-city schools.

The bill was carefully designed and drawn. I drew on the expertise of Reg Gilliam since, as I indicated, he is not only an attorney but a professor of political science as well. We also consulted other educators and educational systems throughout the country about the merits of the bill, and I imagine that some of you here today were contacted while we were getting the bill ready. We drew a great amount of support throughout the country and, if you want further information about that, I would refer you to our hearing record of August 5, 1976. In the House, on HR-14365, you will find statements of support, as well as critical comments on our bill. There was not, of course, unanimous support for the bill. But the intent of the bill was very clear. We wanted to provide direct federal funding so the localities involved in school desegregation disputes would be able to design a full range of remedies for problems encountered in school desegregation. Our hope was that, by increasing available remedies, and by having these additional remedies stress educational methods significantly improving educational quality, we might encourage increased voluntary integration, while reducing mandatory transportation as a means to accomplish desegregation.

Of course, we realize, and we clearly stated this, that our bill in no sense sought to reduce legal authority to correct a constitutional wrong, by whatever means. In fact, our bill was designed to work independently, or in conjunction with transportation orders, as well as to encourage a combination and variety of desegregation methods. In short, we envisioned the bill as a mechanism to fund a full range of programs to help accomplish desegregation, whether court-ordered or not.

Here is a brief description of the features of our bill—features that are novel, positive, and constitutionally sound ways of attacking a problem that has its real roots in segregated housing patterns, job discrimination, unemployment, and other elements beneath the tip of the iceberg we call "school desegregation." (Recall, in this connection the interrelatedness of our modern colonial village...) It is in this context that I cite our original proposal to provide funding to encourage parks and neutral site schools. We thought that, by encouraging building or developing convenient, centrally located schools, or cluster schools, we might then establish more long-term and effective methods of education designed to attract students from different racial backgrounds.

While what finally passed Congress did allow for neutrally-situated schools, it is indeed unfortunate that poorly-articulated fears of so-called "metropolitan area solutions" resulted in the striking out of a clause encouraging more educational parks in traditional feeder patterns in convenient locations. We had better luck in winning authorization for the development of, and operation of, Magnet Schools—schools established on a city-wide basis or within a zone that had specialized educational offerings; that, when well-administered, would prove capable of attracting integrated student bodies—schools like the William Monroe Trotter School in the heart of black Roxbury of the Boston area. Waiting lists last year included 235 white students wanting to get into the school. Whitney Young Magnet School in Chicago opened in 1975, specializing in science, medical arts, and performing arts—three options at one location—and expected to enroll about 2,000 students. In a meeting a couple of days ago with Jesse Jackson, in which we spoke of a whole range of educational options, Jesse spoke happily of the fact that his own daughter had just been accepted into Whitney Young Magnet High School. I might mention that in Chicago the Magnet School concept is beginning to get a great reputation.

Still another example is Houston Technical Institute, which functions as a special purpose high school, drawing students from throughout the city. St. Louis and Boston businesses and institutions of higher education have likewise been deeply involved in carrying out several cooperative magnet programs with local Magnet Schools. As for Cincinnati magnet programs, they have drawn 1,076 students back from private schools. These programs are working!

Dan Levine and Connie Moore of the University of Missouri are in the process of completing a major work in an attempt to determine whether the use of Magnet Schools and magnet programs are indeed as promising and educationally sound as they appear to be. Levine and Moore have identified four prime goals in urban education that Magnets might yet achieve, and which I would like to present to this conference for consideration:

1. Maintaining and improving racial balance in the public schools.

2. Maintaining and improving social and economic balance in the public schools.

3. Improving the opportunity structure for inner-city schools.

4. Contributing to the long-range development of the central city and metropolitan area, particularly through renewal of the inner city and stabilization of integration within communities.

I believe that Magnets can help accomplish these four goals, *if* they are well-administered, and *if* they avoid some of the following pitfalls:

1. Do they merely represent new labels for old programs?

2. Do they draw only the brightest students and best teachers, leaving the remainder of the school system under-resourced? Or are they really a part of a balanced, over-all plan to enrich the entire school system?

3. Are there too many Magnets in a given area, thus diluting the effectiveness of Magnets as schools that draw racially diverse students in significant numbers?

4. Are the Magnets sufficiently tailored and planned so as to be complementary to the neighborhood schools, as well as to the plans of the city as a whole?

We succeeded in winning seventy-five million dollars' authorization over two years in start-up money for this proposal. However, along the way, because of the tortured climate in which we operate in this area, none of the educational issues and questions was addressed. We were told at various stages that there should be no federal involvement in construction; that our bill was a sheep that would be gobbled up by the vocal anti-busing wolves; that our money figure, whether one billion or seventy-five million, was only a drop in the bucket. Yet all of this, all of this emotional turmoil when there are, according to Professor William Taylor of Catholic University Law School, only about 130 school districts in the entire nation involved in school desegregation proceedings! I think it is very reasonable to assume that we can target aid to these areas and that this aid can make a difference. I truly believe we can make a start in doing things that should have been done many, many years ago; things that, if they *had* been done, would have reduced some of the necessity for many of the court-ordered busing decrees we have today.

One of the most disturbing things I found when we got into this whole thing was that HEW, according to its staff, lacked authority to use its planning money, or in fact *any* of its money for many of the activities authorized by S.3319. So, before anyone ridicules the seventy-five million that finally was authorized over a two-year period as being inadequate for the task, let me say this: I think that, even if we had no actual authorization or appropriation money for this bill, we should still find it worthwhile in that it does provide clear legal authority to HEW to use some of its other planning funds for looking into the viability and the feasibility of Magnet Schools across the country. So the bill *has* had that great benefit, quite apart from the direct authorization of dollars that we provided for in the bill itself.

We had difficulty getting through just in terms of discussing problems. I was not on any of the committees directly involved with the bill. I did have good co-sponsors on the bill, people who shared my views. Some of these were Senators Hubert Humphrey of Minnesota, Gary Hart of Colorado, Ted Kennedy of Massachusetts. We did have clout, and used it the best we could. The billion dollar figure scared a lot of people, and I'll tell you, when you get before the Congress *these* days, and you combine the word "billion" with the word "integration," you've got problems! So we didn't get all we would have liked.

We have published a number of articles in the Congressional Record—articles that include testimony from some of you people here today—because it is important to get this information to all parts of the country. We have attempted to make a balanced entry, so some of these articles include views both pro and con on Magnet Schools, neutral sites, and educational parks. I think it very important that Magnet Schools not get lost and go unrecognized. In that spirit, I would like to pay tribute to some of our people in Ohio: to Dr. Don Waldrip, for one, for the noteworthy work he has done in Cincinnati with alternatives and Magnets. And to Dr. Paul Briggs in Cleveland, who has also done excellent work in this field.

My primary goal is quality education for our nation's young people; and, in that context, Magnet Schools constitute a very long stride on a very long avenue in the right direction. I am aware, too, that some communities in earlier years used Magnets for reasons not limited to integration, but for the educational excellence they provide. This excellence they can continue to offer, quite apart from the issue of integration. And now, in our time, they can also provide a very much needed alternative to mandatory transportation, which so upsets some people in our society.

The great advantage of Magnet Schools today is that they enable many Americans to voluntarily achieve the goal of integrated, quality education on a hitherto unprecedented scale. That is why I have involved myself in this issue after only a little more than two years in Washington. I consider the enactment of the School Integration Innovation Act a matter of real pride and importance, and a vehicle by which we can all travel toward the great goals we have set for ourselves and for American education.

The Revolution in Technical Education and
Its Impact on the Concept of Educational Options

3

The Revolution in Technical Education and Its Impact on the Concept of Educational Options

B. FRANK BROWN

Introduction

Calling formal education as we know it today, "an aging vat for youth," Dr. Frank Brown asks that "education and work become joint components in the total educational process," and that youth "have the opportunity of multiple-entry choice." He then discusses at length the "nation's new policy toward youth," which will emphasize jobs and voluntary participation, while noting that "there is considerable support for a compulsory youth service."

In his play, *King Richard III,* Shakespeare has the young Duke of Gloucester say, "Now is the winter of our discontent." If a modern-day Shakespeare were writing about the current problems of education, he would probably begin, "Now is the winter, spring, summer, and fall of our discontent!"

There is, perhaps, more disillusionment about education abroad in the land than at any time in the past. The epitome of this discontent has culminated in Grand Jury investigations into school discipline in some districts, and the closing of schools in others.

Kenneth Boulding, a professor at the University of Colorado, has expressed the current agonies of the schools better than anyone else. According to Boulding, "The proposition that education is a declining industry is well-known by this time . . . and declining industries are rarely innovators because they suffer from the increasing dead weight of the past. Past commitments form a larger proportion of the annual budgets. The sheer maintenance of the system seems to take all of its resources."

If we accept Professor Boulding's analysis, then we can expect the secondary schools to become much less innovative than they were in the past, and that general education will continue to decline.

It is a tribute, then, to technical education that, unlike general education, it is steadily growing in strength. In fact, though it was born in private schools *outside* of the educational mainstream, it is increasingly being recognized as having a significant role to play in the field of public education. The truth of the matter is that technical education has become so critical in American life that C.P. Snow's term, a "literary culture," no longer really defines the educational process. For, as we continue to approach a state of "techno-merit-ocracy," it is clear that literary learning must be supplemented by more than just a smattering of technical knowledge if our youth are to be considered truly and fully educated.

From the time when the high schools first moved into the area of technical education, they have been playing an important role in preparing their students to become technicians. This development has grown to the point where many secondary schools are becoming community-based as they increase the options available to students; similarly, technical education is rapidly spilling over from high school vocational departments into community businesses.

In spite of the advances which have been made in vocational and technical education, it is important to recognize that there is still a long way to go. More than one-third of the vocational school graduates are still being trained for agriculture or home economics. This should be a signal to schools that they must move more rapidly into other service and technical areas.

The key to a greatly expanded alternatives program is the development of truly collaborative processes between the schools and community-based institutions. We have passed the era in which schools and community-based educational programs are equal, but separate, forces. Instead, there are now major efforts being made throughout the United States to bring the two together and to have them work jointly in the training of our youth.

Educational planners have minimized the fundamental changes in structure, organization, methodology, and human relationships which a change to alternative programs requires. As secondary schools have moved to alternatives, they have included in their curricula a wide-ranging system of alternatives which offer a meaningful educational choice to every student. With proper guidance, each adolescent is able to select the form of schooling and learning most congenial to his or her basic learning style, philosophical orientation, and taste.

The chief difficulty with the existing system of formal education is the single-point i.e., kindergarten or first grade (1) entry followed by sequential promotions from grade one to two to three . . . to twelve. These twin locksteps tend to make formal education "an aging vat" for youth. However, as education and work become joint components in the total educational process, youth will have the opportunity of multiple-entry choice.

The advantage of such a multiple-entry program (*i.e.,* combining work and schooling) is that the education of the young becomes the active responsibility of society as a whole, rather than simply the function of a small sub-system called the school. Though the latter will of course remain a fundamental component in the education of youth, it must become a partner of the community, since an increasing amount of young people's education will take place in the world of work.

Through a new mix of school and community resources, alternative education programs have developed new delivery systems, as well as innovative approaches to the traditional structure of the credit hour, the classroom, and the semester schedule. This development has grown out of the notion that a considerable part of the educational process should be based upon community needs and should take place in the "classroom" of the community.

A characteristic of technical education, which makes it highly appropriate to community-based learning, is that a great deal of it falls into the category of "learning in the workplace."

Recent research into the preparation for technical jobs reveals that about half the craftsmen and foremen in the United States have had no formal occupational training. This data gives support to the belief that community-based learning will provide a more satisfactory basis for a career in a technical area.

What alternative education has done is to change the image of the secondary schools. While secondary schools used to be idyllic ponds or communes, splendid in their isolation from the rest of society, they are now educational institutions firmly committed to community-based education. Through alternative programs and options, the high schools are offering significant learning style options to students and, at the same time, providing them with a milieu that is suited to their personal lives and growing patterns.

Among their other achievements, alternative programs in education have revolutionized the ways we deal with youth. Specifically, they have eliminated the kinds of isolation found in traditional schools which has so often alienated young people from adult society. At the same time, they have helped young people make an orderly and effective transition from childhood to a constructive participation in adult life.

When alternative programs were first initiated, many of their supporters feared that they might be equated with undue permissiveness or lack of structure. These fears have proved idle, however. Though some alternative schools offer students almost complete freedom in their educational tasks, others are highly structured (i.e., based on considerable external discipline and direction). And, whatever their differences, they have all emphasized sound educational experiences for young people.

An important side effect of the innovation of alternatives has been the elimination of the instant curriculum remedies of the 50's and 60's. Alternatives have illustrated the fact that these were indeed naive approaches to complex educational problems. Unfortunately, though, such "remedies" made the public skeptical about all school innovation, and this has been a major hurdle that alternatives have had to face.

Without realizing, perhaps, that they were developing in fact a national model, leaders of the alternatives and options movement created new contexts for youth by giving them broader exposure to the world of work and by easing their transition into the labor market. These accomplishments are currently being recognized by Congress and are being viewed within the framework of a national model that offers new environments for youth.

A New National Policy Toward Youth

Up to the present time, society has relied upon the secondary schools as the major institution for serving youth. There is now a strong Congressional movement afoot to create new environments designed to assist youth in its transition to adulthood. Leadership in this effort is coming from the Carter/Mondale administration, which, out of concern that youth have jobs, has placed the establishment of a youth policy and legislation for a National Youth Service high among its priorities.

This represents a radical departure from the past, when the only national policy toward youth was one of reaction, rather than action. Such passive policies resulted only in short-term palliatives, when what was sorely needed was an ongoing national policy directed at the problems of youth.

The new federal activity is being fanned by the aggravation of unemployment and crime among our youth. Unemployment, for example, is currently running at twenty percent for young people overall, and forty percent for Black youth. In addition, there is growing evidence that juvenile delinquency has a direct relation to the level of unemployment among the young. For this reason legislators are especially disturbed by the rapid acceleration in the numbers of crimes committed by adolescents. Between 1960 and 1974, juvenile arrests jumped by a whopping 138 percent, while in 1976, fourteen out of every hundred juveniles committed a crime for which they were arrested. The arrests of juveniles for violent crimes have almost tripled. Within ten years, we have gone from one arrest per 400 juveniles to one arrest for every 140 juveniles. Persons under eighteen now account for nearly fifty percent of all arrests for serious crimes. These statistics alone are more than enough justification for urgent Congressional action toward creating new and better environments for youth.

An analysis of the bills which are being introduced by such powerful figures as Senators Humphrey, Jackson, Javits, and Cranston indicates that, within a very short time, some kind of national policy toward youth will be legislated. This policy will probably take two forms: (1) a National Service for Youth and (2) a meaningful job program which emphasizes skills development combined with the performance of useful services within the local community.

Much of this Congressional reasoning is based on the premise that compulsory military service, which formerly served as a major vehicle for assisting young people in their transition from youth to adulthood, no longer exists. With this option now closed, and with seventy percent of all employers not hiring anyone below the age of twenty-one, the result is a massive exclusion of young people from jobs. Incidentally, most of the current Congressional proposals advocate that the National Youth Service be voluntary, but there is considerable support (as well as justification) for a *compulsory* youth service.

Among the major youth issues that Congress is increasingly concerned about are:

- New programs for the socialization of youth
- The successful transition of youth from school to work
- Expanding community service for youth
- National service for youth

- Increased employment opportunities for out-of-school youth
- Decreased criminal activities of youth
- The development of new forms of education for that segment of youth which cannot master the basic tools for learning.

The legislation which seems most likely to pass the Congress in the near future will give young people the opportunity to choose between serving in their home communities or joining conservation programs in a state or federal park. Yet, whatever legislation comes, it is clear that school programs of options and alternatives will be profoundly influenced by such Congressional action. The new question being asked about young people is not "How much schooling should they have?" but, "What are the appropriate environments in which they can make the transition into adulthood smoothly?" And performing community service while learning employment skills clearly ranks high among the alternatives which Congress is now considering.

While the specific content of the new federal legislation is being developed, identical themes are seen in both the proposed Senate and House bills. Basically, the new programs for youth would involve:

- A major commitment to assist poorly prepared youth in becoming productively employed
- A strong emphasis on their performing useful work in the community
- The opportunity for youth to acquire new job skills from a host of options and alternatives.

It should be emphasized here that the current mood of Congress is not to establish a special or emergency program for youth, but rather to create a regular and ongoing one. While this *basic* commitment will be public, the private sector — including both business and organized labor — will also have a significant role to play in the creation of these new options and alternatives for youth.

What are the implications for the secondary schools of these new federal programs? Clearly, those secondary schools which are already operating alternative programs will be greatly expanded under the nation's new policy toward youth. Since these alternative programs use the community as an alternative classroom, the new federal programs will find in them a ready-made model on which to base similar programs for youth.

The Importance of Work in the Successful Transition of Youth to Adulthood

In the past, very little attention was paid to the role that work could have in assuring young people a smooth transition from youth to adulthood. This is surprising, since research into the meaning of work has indicated that it may well be the single most significant factor in guaranteeing that this transition is effectively made.

In a major study, Freedman and Havighurst determined that work has the following functions:

- To provide income
- To afford a meaningful expenditure of time and energy
- To create identification and status
- To create meaningful personal associations
- To be a source of meaningful life experiences.

When we add to the above two other functions which are important to the individual (to promote self-respect and the respect for others, and to help one to express oneself creatively), it is clear that work is critical in this transition process.

Finally, since work is the activity around which most people organize their daily experiences and establish a productive and rewarding routine, it must loom large in any governmental effort to improve the condition of young people. One has only to view the lives of men without work — and the absence of a sense of purpose which people have when they do not have work — to understand the critical importance of employment, particularly in a work-oriented culture such as ours.

(It is interesting to note here that other industrialized nations are not having our problems largely because their youth have not been faced with the critical issue of unemployment.)

It should be clear by now that a variety of experiences must be introduced into the lives of young people to assist them in the difficult transition from youth to adulthood. With this in mind, it should be equally evident that the first priority of a federal national policy is to set up work/study programs for young people between the ages of fourteen and twenty-one. The work portion of this combined program should take the form of a community internship, which should guarantee students a minimum wage. In short, the goal would be to provide young people with employment and, at the same time, give them the opportunity to perform meaningful services in their communities for which they would be remunerated.

SUMMARY

In recent years, we have increasingly come to realize that work and education are not opposing forces, and that an individual should not have to choose one or the other at a particular stage in his life. Rather, we recognize the fact that they are complementary processes, and that the emphasis placed on each will vary according to an individual's needs and his stage of life. Most likely, there will continue to be a greater emphasis on education and a lesser one on work in the earlier ages of youth, and just the reverse of this as one grows older. But neither should educational work ever be entirely excluded from any stage of life.

In short, we must abandon our traditional obsession and exclusive dependence on a formal system of education. Instead, a whole range of possibilities for informal learning is emerging whose intent is to bring young people into earlier touch with adults and adult activities, thus enabling them to enter into what is called "functional participation." This can become possible only when the program of informal education is woven around work experiences situated in the local community.

In the near future, educators can expect new federal legislation and federal policy to provide for a massive expansion of alternatives and community-based education for youth. As the country begins to grapple with the problems of its jobless, discriminated-against, and unskilled youth, it is apparent that community-based options and alternatives offer the best possibility of achieving the twin goals of full employment and a meaningful adult life for the young people of our country.

Alternatives: Strategies for Getting Started

4

Alternatives: Strategies for Getting Started

JOHN B. DAVIS, JR. and MARGE HOLS

Introduction

In the following pages, Dr. Davis and Ms. Hols discuss the nature of the change in education and the strategies for bringing it about. Dr. Davis draws heavily on his experiences as a large-city superintendent while offering a thorough, practical description of a basic model for initiating a system of alternatives.

There is strong evidence that alternatives are education's future direction. The current literature as well as the advocacy of concerned educators and parents signal that education will become oriented toward option and choice.

The traditional school approach to teaching and learning has been allowed to eclipse all others in most American public schools. This situation continues despite declining achievement scores, an increase in dropouts, discipline problems, and parent, student, and community dissatisfaction. But if public schools are to provide environments and instruction appropriate and adequate for everyone (which is the public's expectation), they must move out of the paths of habit and begin to offer more options.

What dynamics are necessary to upset the status quo in the interest of better and more varied learning opportunities for students of all ages? What must be done to assure more participation and involvement in the multiple processes of public education and meet the infinite variety of children's needs?[1]

As public schools across the nation seek answers to these questions, their goal must be "alternatives." Alternative programs are a proven route to comprehensive school change and to increased satisfaction on the part of students, parents, and teachers.[2] This is because alternatives make sense. So long as there is diversity among students and teachers, there must not be one way, but many alternate ways to learn.

Implementing alternatives as a prescription for educational reform requires comprehensive changes in public schools. The school district climate must give preference to variability over standardization, decentralization over centralization, diversity over conformity, cooperation over competition, flexibility over rigidity. There must be tolerance for a multiplicity of goals rather than for a single purpose. Above all, there must be loyalty to the concept that the schools belong to the

47

people, and that the people should be involved in how their children are taught and what they should learn.

These conclusions are drawn from the real world of public school administration, with particular reference to what has been accomplished in the Minneapolis public schools over the past decade.

Why Minneapolis as a model for change? Because, in recent years, the Minneapolis schools have taken major steps to desegregate, decentralize, implement systemwide alternatives, turn around declining achievement scores, address racism and sexism openly, develop a multi-ethnic curriculum, expand services to exceptional children, and build a community education program involving more than 100,000 participants. These changes have significantly improved the quality of education in Minneapolis schools.[3]

Why Minneapolis as a model for alternatives? Because more than 15,000 of Minneapolis' 25,000 elementary students now attend alternative schools (mainly open, modified open, continuous progress, modified traditional, or traditional) which they and their parents chose.

The Minneapolis Southeast Alternatives (SEA) Project is recognized nationally as a successful experiment in offering alternatives within the public school system. The Minneapolis School Board led the nation in 1973 by mandating that every elementary student should have a choice other than the traditional program by 1976. Alternatives are also developing in Minneapolis secondary schools, though more slowly, as the demand for continuous progress and open schools percolates and as students comfortable with these programs enter the junior and senior high schools. There are, for example, a K-12 free school, a K-12 open school program, a K-8 open school, and several 6-8 continuous progress programs. Additionally, many junior and senior highs have pocket schools-within-a-school, or alternative schools in separate locations. A common trimester schedule allows secondary students to move between schools to reach a broader range of subjects than any single "comprehensive high school" could offer. Finally, cooperative arrangement with the Federation of Alternative Schools, a group of nonpublic schools, provides additional choice for some secondary students who would not or could not respond to public school requirements.

Basic Requirements for School Change

What factors should educators consider in judging the potential for comprehensive change in their own settings via alternatives? Yale University's Seymour B. Sarason has written that school systems attempting to solve their own problems must begin by understanding the basics of change. In the public schools, the problem is how to change an ongoing school so that it will reflect new and different ideas. The solution, he says, is to change life in the school and in the classroom.[4]

Sarason suggests that one possible dilemma the would-be reformer might have would be "where to start," because the minimal conditions required for change are not present. "Then the challenge becomes — what changes have to take place before the minimal conditions exist?"[5]

Let's review here some "minimal conditions" necessary for effective school change, drawn from the authors' experience.

1. Although an all-out crisis isn't necessary, there must be at least a climate of overhanging uncertainty and an acknowledged dissatisfaction with the status quo, coupled with the belief that the schools should — and could — be improved.

2. The school board must understand the need for change — the need to move out of paths of educational habit which no longer best serve particular groups of students. Ideally, the board should lead, and the community should sense the board's leadership role. Once commitment to new directions has been made, the board must support the superintendent, principals, teachers, and staff as plans are developed and steps toward change are taken. The board must allow administrators to make decisions without laying their jobs on the line. Teachers, principals, and parents must be encouraged and sustained by recognition and approval.

3. Time – years of time – must be allowed to accomplish comprehensive change. A realistic time perspective must be established and understood by all participants.

4. The planning process must be carefully devised so that those who will be affected understand and can participate in setting goals and planning activities. This, of course, is a tall order and can never be accomplished fully, given the nature of school bureaucracy. Nonetheless, it is essential that faculty and staff have opportunities to participate in the planning and designing stages; if they do not, the program probably will fail. Others also affected must be involved, including clerical personnel, parents, and the students for whom the effort is being made. Each of these groups must be encouraged to participate in the governance of any innovation. Governance is key to sustained effort. Responsibility, risk, and consequences of failure must be on the shoulders of many, not exclusively on those of educators and administrators.

5. Support and in-service training opportunities for the new tasks which these changes will impose must be provided in nonthreatening ways to administrators and teachers. Whenever possible, parents should be permitted to take part in training programs.

6. There must be a sufficient budget to support internal and external communications, specialsts and consultants, in-service staff development, and evaluation procedures used in distinguishing between what is, was, and shall be. Obtaining funds from outside sources is preferable, since this allows for greater risk-taking.

7. Superintendent and school board must understand something about the various categories of change, including the most important one; namely, that which alters a fundamental process through sharing power and authority. Changes do not always occur smoothly or inevitably. New ideas, arrangements, emphases, and allocations of precious human and financial resources can threaten existing

programs and upset even well-intentioned personnel.[6] Demands of an existing program also can retard change.

Sarason has observed that when a change involves a large part of a school system, its fate will in some measure be determined by the discrepancy in that system between proposals made and proposals implemented, particularly if the promoters of change are unaware of this discrepancy. In other words, success breeds success; inaction breeds failure.[7]

In many ways, it might be easier to stop everything and start all over again, but the "easy way" is impractical. Evolution, not revolution, is the course of our political system — *i.e.,* to modify, adapt, expand, enlarge, and yet to keep some of the old as the new is developed. Teachers, principals, and superintendents, with the support of an understanding school board, therefore must propose, illustrate, and argue convincingly how change can be accomplished, and to what end. Only then should they attempt to secure sanction from colleagues and parents.

8. A final critical requirement for change is to recognize that changes in education today depend heavily on the political climate. Social progress, as George Orwell observed, has not and will not occur simply because of humanitarian outpourings by individuals or organizations. Rather, it comes from hard-fought, usually radical positions which, along with compromise, are reflected ultimately in legislation, judicial review, and executive fiat.

What this means is that everyone involved in public education must be an activist. An important aspect of this activist role is in the political arena. A partnership between educators and legislators is essential. With educators lies the key to broad local discretion in meeting individual educational needs; with legislators, the authority and responsibility to provide adequate financing and support. State departments of education also need assistance. They need to hear from those who are close to the educational problems and opportunities to be found at the school level, where children and teachers meet.

The Scouts-Out Approach to Change

A rigid system cannot all of a sudden embark on a massive plan for total change. First, there have to be new systems of delivery of educational programs, and new visions of parent and community participation and direction.

A district must begin with models for change; not just one model, but many launched at the same time. A big school system cannot be changed by announcing a target, then by lining up the troops like redcoats, and charging ahead. Instead, it must get the scouts out — to capture a piece of land, and then to change it, modify it, adapt it, to ensure that it serves the stated purpose. In short, there has to be simultaneous activity — and a lot of it — on many fronts. If everyone is working on a single plan at the same time, it may be disastrous, because all the forces opposing change can unify and intensify their sabotage efforts.

There is a lesson to be emphasized in the "scouts-out" strategy. Do it well somewhere in a school, in an area, and there will be a demand for its replication in another school or area. Do it poorly somewhere or everywhere, on the other hand, and ridicule and rejection are likely to follow!

Each school system wishing to implement alternatives must begin with a model. Although successful national models exist, such as the Minneapolis Southeast Alternatives (SEA) Project, and though much can be learned from their experiences, nothing takes the place of a successful model which can be used locally to define what is meant by alternatives, and to test in a nonthreatening way the community's capacity for a range of alternatives.

Fail-Safe Model for Alternative Schools

The Minneapolis Southeast Alternatives (SEA) Project began in September, 1971, as one of the first three national Experimental Schools Projects (ESPs) funded by the U.S. Office of Education. Over the next five years, it received $6.6 million in federal funds. ESPs were established to test business/industry's input-output model for productivity; they also were designed to get educational research off paper and into practice, and to achieve comprehensive school change via systems planning.

The area chosen for the SEA experiment was Southeast Minneapolis, the home of factories, railroad yards, residential areas, housing projects, flour mills, shopping areas, and the main campus of the University of Minnesota. The 30,000 Southeast residents represent a diverse range of life styles, income levels, and educational backgrounds, and are predominantly white.

In 1971, Southeast Minneapolis public schools served about 2,200 of the city school system's 65,000 students. About 10.5 percent of the Southeast students were from minority ethnic groups.

For the five project years, SEA became a separate, decentralized administrative unit of the school district.·Under SEA, what previously had been four traditional neighborhood elementary schools and a junior-senior high school became a single attendance area. Families now chose between contemporary (modified traditional), continuous progress, open, and free school programs. Elementary programs and the free school are housed in separate buildings. Three secondary programs are housed in the junior-senior high school.

Lessons learned from the SEA model which probably are transferable to other school districts include the following:

1. There must be one or more constituencies within the system expressing the wish to have an alternative program. Ideally, there would be a constituency of parents and teachers.

Attempts at change are much more effective when the district adjusts to external demands, rather than when it initiates and implements changes independently. Unless the district is pressured, it is much more difficult for teachers, administrators, and school board members to realize the importance of modification and change. Demand for change from parents and students can, of course, be fostered by school personnel.

Administrative response to pressure should be cautious but encouraging, resulting in a balance between the demands of clients on the one hand, and accommodations by the school district on the other. If the clients' demands for change are refused, their only recourse is revolution or withdrawal from the system. Dynamic tension in the community must be permitted to exist; otherwise, there will be no commitment or feeling of accomplishment on the part of those involved.

Southeast Minneapolis parents and teachers had been pressuring the school district to offer alternatives since the late 1960's. In 1970, the attendance areas of two Southeast Minneapolis schools were combined in a "pairing" arrangement. One school served all K-3 students from both school areas, and began offering a continuous progress program (the system's second). The other school served all the 4-6 students, and planned to convert to a continuous progress program the following year, 1971.

Another group, Parents for Open Classrooms, had extracted from the superintendent a commitment for at least one "open" classroom (the system's first) within a Southeast elementary school by fall 1971.

Finally, the Southeast area junior-senior high school, which had merged with the nearby University of Minnesota high school in 1968, already had responded to demands for a less structured program for a small group of students by creating an in-house alternative program — the School Without Walls.

2. Participants must work toward a definition of an alternative program. This is easier said than done, because alternatives are amorphous, and each alternative program takes its character from those it serves.

This issue never has been settled in Minneapolis, although the School Board adopted an official policy definition in 1975. The latter is still being debated, disputed, and defended by the city's parents, teachers, and administrators.

While the original Southeast Alternatives plan did not define an alternative program formally, it did provide for (a) choice-making by parents, students, and teachers; (b) multiple instructional patterns, each with separate identity and a full curriculum; and (c) faculty, parent, and student participation in governance.[8]

The school district's Task Force on Alternatives, appointed by the superintendent early in 1973, adopted "seven ground rules for alternative schools" which were adapted from Mario Fantini's book, *Public Schools of Choice*.[9] The ground rules stated that an alternative school has comprehensive educational objectives; does not increase per pupil expenditure substantially; does not advocate any racial, religious, or economic exclusivity; is not imposed; must respect the rights of all; does not claim to be *the* answer; and advocates a process of change which is democratic and maximizes individual decision-making.[10]

In 1974, the Task Force on Alternatives adopted a five-point definition of an alternative program, which the SEA director adapted from the State Education Department of New York's definition.[11] This defined an alternative program as a full comprehensive program; stylistically different and physically distinct from other programs; available by choice to students, parents, teachers, and administrators; a program involving the community it serves in its decision-making and in its developmental processes of planning, implementation, and evaluation; a program that allows its students to progress with continuity and consistency from the elementary through the secondary level.[12]

(The official policy on alternatives adopted by the School Board in 1975 is identical to the above, except that the requirement for a full comprehensive program has been eliminated.)[13]

3. The clients must decide which alternatives they want. Teachers, students, parents, and administrators must work together to determine the range of alternatives required to meet all perceived needs. Any parent choice, so long as there is sufficient support, becomes a possibility, so long as it is educationally sound, and is judged to fall within the framework of state and constitutional limits and local board policies.

The SEA planning group decided that the Southeast Minneapolis community had "customers" for contemporary (slightly freer than traditional), continuous progress, open, and free schools. Traditional and continuous progress schools were already in operation, and an open program was about to begin. Planners also agreed that each alternative should be housed in a separate building. This meant that small programs, such as a proposed Montessori classroom, could not be accommodated.[14]

There was less agreement on secondary alternatives. The proposal described a single junior-senior high school, offering "an eclectic curriculum, but centered around four instructional modes in the expectation that continuing student, parent, and faculty interaction will generate the relevant curriculum offerings at any given point."[15]

The decision to include a free school resulted from strong pressure by some school administrators and parents who felt that a broad range of choices should be offered in an experimental program. A second reason for the decision was an increasing amount of disruptive behavior and a consequent increase in the number of high school dropouts. This condition was in part attributed to discontent with the high school program, as well as with the school environment.

As alternatives have spread to other Minneapolis schools, many continuous progress, open, modified open, and modified traditional schools have been established. The SEA Free School has not been emulated elsewhere; one reason for this may be that it draws its enrollment citywide, and has expanded from 67 to 176 students over five years. Recently, the seeds of parent demand for a fundamentals school have surfaced in two areas. Although no such public school currently exists in the city, a proposal by the superintendent to begin a fundamentals school in the fall is being discussed. (Two fundamental schools were opened in September 1977.)

The Minneapolis school district also has developed increasingly sophisticated procedures for determining the range of alternatives desired by the community. In answer to the School Board's 1973 mandate that every elementary student must have access to an alternative program by 1976, each of the three decentralized districts of the school system formulated plans. Each district plan was different, in keeping with the requirement that programs be developed in response to community needs. However, the sequencing of the process — surveying, planning, implementing, evaluating — was common to all the plans. So was community participation. Parent questionnaires and staff surveys were developed to determine the demand for a range of alternatives in each cluster of schools.[16]

One happy and frequently overlooked outcome of the alternatives system in Minneapolis is that the *traditional* school becomes a viable option when the student has a choice. Those considering alternatives are cautioned that they must not proceed by attacking the legitimacy of the traditional school; rare would be the community without a powerful constituency in support of such schools!

4. The goals of the project must be clearly stated, understood, and agreed upon by as many participants as possible. At the outset of the SEA project, the School Board and administration declared that no alternative programs could lose sight of the fundamental purpose for which schools are maintained and the standards they are judged by: *i.e.*, the attainment of basic communication, computational, and problem-solving skills. This fundamental purpose became a ''given'' for *all* alternative programs.

Widespread knowledge of, and agreement on, SEA goals developed during the project years. These goals included providing a curriculum which helps children master basic skills; offering educational options within a public school setting which support individual differences for all involved in the educational process; enabling students, teachers, and parents to make choices among five major program options; emphasizing student development in the affective, as well as cognitive domain; exploring decentralized governance involving parents, faculty, students, and administrators; testing, over a five-year period, a comprehensive K-12 plan to reform education, involving the use of many promising practices and products of research.[17]

(Although the SEA schools became Magnet Schools that attracted minority students from other parts of the city and resulted in improved racial balances, desegregation was not an original project goal.)

5. Parent involvement is key to the success of any alternative program. All parents must get involved because they must choose a program for each child.

For an alternative program to work, it must have advocates with a stake in the project, and that stake must be the children. Good and respected as the faculty may be, nothing is as persuasive as the warm word of one parent to another about the wholesomeness of the program and his or her confidence in it. In other words, there must be an ''outreach,'' an assurance from one parent to the next that the alternative program is O.K. and that it may be better than a program a child has been in, depending on the child's needs and learning style.

The project must build a communications network that reaches every parent in the project community. SEA accomplished this feat during the first year by direct contact — much of it parent-to-parent. Frank Reynolds, who evaluated the Minneapolis project, summarized this achievement in a final report to the National Institute of Education (NIE).

Committees of paid and volunteer parents sent out flyers and brochures, tracked down addresses, assisted with neighborhood and PTA orientations, compiled tables of responses and conducted phone campaigns. The goal that every parent must make a choice was met before school opened, with a small group of parents contacting the last few families by door-to-door canvassing.

By the close of the first year, the public information component of SEA had started a community newspaper, developed a slide show, and accommodated visitors. Assistance from individuals or committees of parents, volunteering to conduct special tours and orientations, continued. Families contemplating choice were urged to visit the existing alternative programs, where an orientation was conducted by counselors, community liaisons, teachers and principals . . . .[18]

The second year, choice cards were mailed by each school to all families who visited schools during a designated visiting week. In addition to this formal approach, presentations to PTAs, school conferences, brochures, phone calls, school visits and 'the grapevine' — talking to other parents and attending community meetings — were contacts influencing choicemaking.

By the fourth project year, choice cards were mailed only to parents who wished to initiate a transfer of schools for the next academic year. Both formal and informal school selection processes had become sufficiently routinized for that to happen. . . .[19]

Another evaluation showed that the informal mechanisms of school visits and talks to other parents were by far the most potent information mechanisms for

The percent of elementary families choosing an SEA alternative program which meant travel beyond the school nearest their residence increased steadily during the project years, from twenty-eight, to thirty-one, to forty-seven, and then to fifty percent by the fourth year. SEA's Magnet appeal is reflected clearly in these figures. The first project year, only three percent of the elementary students in SEA schools came from other parts of the city; by the fourth year, twenty-five percent did. Because many of the transfer students from outside SEA were from minority families, the minority student percentage in SEA elementary schools increased from 10.5 percent in 1970 to twenty-one percent in 1974.[21]

From SEA [Minneapolis evaluator Larry Johnson concluded] the Minneapolis system learned that, when given sufficient information, parents will select a school other than the one closest to their home in order to get the appropriate alternative program for their children. It also learned — which was important for the concurrent desegregation program — that there is not a significant difference between the interest of minority and majority groups when alternative programs are offered following valid parent participation in development of the programs.

Minneapolis parents, within and beyond SEA, have embraced the concept of alternatives in unexpected numbers. For example, more than seventy-five percent of 2,000 parents of randomly selected West Area district students surveyed in 1975 said that having alternative educational programs provided was important to them . . . .

Among elementary parents, thirty-eight percent were willing to have their children transported to any school in the West Area to get the program of their choice; forty-three percent were willing to have their child transported to the next closest school to their child's present school; while only nineteen percent said they would choose the nearest available school, regardless of program offered.[22]

6. *It does not seem likely that an alternative program comprehensive in nature would be possible in the absence of a strong central administrator who has widespread support.*

In Minneapolis, the superintendent was backed not only by the School Board and faculty, but also had broad-based community support from business, labor, the news media, and the city's power structure. He was able and willing to debate and defend his educational positions, having come to the city with an impressive record of achievements in a variety of undertakings, including public school administration. His public statements were planned carefully, prepared, and frequent enough to command attention, and his staff was remarkably supportive and intelligent.

7. *The model project must be autonomous, with a decentralized administrative structure, and administrators must have power to make necessary changes without undue interference from "central office" administrators or the school board.*

The superintendent must liberate talented administrators and teachers from their regular duties so that they can work with parents and students to find new ways to plan and implement the project. The project director is the key to success and must be a person who can find and encourage other school leaders to action at many grade levels. He or she also must be able to delegate authority, be happy with uncertainty, and have a very high tolerance for differences in other people's life styles.

Energy is essential! Administrators must make tough demands on colleagues and get increased production beyond their normal routine of work. Once people are immersed in a project, they want to make it work; the job itself usually becomes increasingly absorbing; and less and less outside push becomes necessary.

In 1970, the principal of the Southeast junior-senior high school was freed from his regular duties to head proposal development for the Experimental Schools Project (ESP). Five months and thousands of working hours later, when the ESP federal grant was assured, he was appointed by the superintendent to the position of SEA project director and invited to join the superintendent's staff cabinet. At that point, the area of the city embracing the Southeast schools was part of the centralized administrative structure, although some schools in two other areas of the city had been organized into "pyramids," governed by an area administrator, with expanded local authority and discretionary power.

The lesson learned in SEA's first months was that the project director must have status and power to bring about comprehensive change. In January 1972, the superintendent issued a statement instructing the five SEA principals to report henceforth directly to the SEA project director. He further ordered that allotments in budget and personnel would no longer go from the central office to individual school principals but would be delegated instead to the project director.[23]

The superintendent's scouts-out strategy contributed to SEA autonomy. SEA was only one of many simultaneous innovations underway in the Minneapolis schools. Another innovation was the beginning of a model project for racial desegregation in 1971 which involved the first mandatory movement of students. Concurrently, there was a move toward citywide administrative decentralization, including a requirement that each school have an active advisory council of teachers and parents. Other innovations included progress toward a network of community education councils; direct liaison with nonpublic alternative, inner-city, store-front schools; a multi-ethnic curriculum; Indian education programs; models for mainstreaming special education students, and a variety of secondary alternatives programs. The effect of all this was to defuse opposition to educational change and to create many small and large support groups.

   8. The alternative model must provide real opportunities for community self-governance.

   SEA's structure evolved over the five project years into a reasonable model for self-governance. The opportunities created for SEA parent and teacher participation in decision-making (within the framework of central School Board policy and state education guidelines) were unusual, if not unique in public education.

   For example, each school has a parent and faculty screening committee which interviews prospective teachers and principals, and makes recommendations to the personnel department. Parents choose which school each of their children will attend. (Parents get their first choice, which they may change later, if they wish, after a parent-teacher conference.)

   During the project years, the Teacher Center In-Service Committee has decided how to spend several hundred thousand dollars of curriculum and staff development funds. Decisions about individual school budgets have been made by each school's governance group, working with the principal. Although the principal has authority over funds allocated to each school, in practice he or she works with the group from the outset, so that the final decision is a joint one.

   Of course, this level of shared participation, responsibility, and authority did not happen overnight. The director's efforts to convert the university-school district policy board operating the SEA high school to the SEA project policy board were rejected by central office administrators. During the first project year, the director held weekly meetings with key project staff. By January 1972, the superintendent had approved formation of a strong advisory group, the Southeast Community Education Council. Agreement on its powers was reached, with the superintendent delegating broad authority within School Board policy. The council began interviewing candidates for staff positions, and making recommendations to the director on a broad range of SEA project operations.[24]

   An SEA management team headed by the project director was created the following year. It was composed of principals and the heads of staff development, internal evaluation, community education, and student support services. This team provided decision-making leadership in project planning, policy-making, and operations. SEA's fourth year passed with the management team and community council discussing a merger. This led to creation of a unified Southeast Community Council/SEA Management Team, consisting of school district staff and parents, which began operations in SEA's fifth year.[25]

Parents participated in the governance of each of the SEA schools, as well as in government of the project. The final SEA evaluation report said that parents of children at the contemporary school were highly satisfied with a PTA advisory structure, whereas open school parents were satisfied with bi-weekly three-hour planning meetings with the principal. From SEA, it was learned that ''community satisfaction with involvement in school affairs is not dependent on any one type of participation.'' Almost all parents had some ''zones of indifference'' — i.e., areas they perceived to be the responsibility of principal or teacher — although these zones were different for each school.[26]

This parent participation in governance accomplished three things, according to the report. First, it provided a public forum to explain what had been done, how, and why. Second, the public received an education in the complexities of administering public education. And, last, it led to greater consumer satisfaction and sense of control in the public schools, while maintaining respect for teachers and principals.[27]

9. *Staff development opportunities are critical.* At the outset, teachers and administrators must be given the option of staying in project schools or of transferring to schools outside the project area. Those who choose to remain must be allowed to choose their alternative program, and must be afforded nonthreatening opportunities for planning and retraining. These opportunities should be made available without making either teachers or administrators feel incompetent, ill-prepared, unknowing, or dull. Continuing opportunities for such retraining must exist throughout the project years.

One SEA innovation in this area was the development of a Teacher Center to provide the retraining which faculty needed to function more effectively either in their present positions or in new and unfamiliar ones. The center's initial charge was to meet the training needs of both faculty and parents, and to involve them in providing a number of alternatives at elementary and secondary levels. Later, the center became the Minneapolis Public Schools/University of Minnesota (MPS/UM) Teacher Center. Operating with joint funds, it began to participate in new curriculum development at both school and university levels, blending pre-service and in-service training. It also provided new roles for teachers and community people via temporary assignments and internships to the center which ranged from six weeks to a year.

Teacher centers weren't invented in Minneapolis. The unique feature of the MPS/UM Teacher Center, according to its director, is that each individual determines what it is that he or she needs to learn to be part of a changing educational institution. By submitting a brief proposal to a board of their peers, teachers may obtain funds for this training. This training model encourages risk-taking, because no one has to admit professional deficiency to some superior in the administrative structure. In Minneapolis, the Teacher Center provides such training opportunities for instructional, supervisory, and administrative staff of alternative schools.[28]

There are times when a school's organizational structure may discourage teachers from discussing classroom difficulties with their principal, since it is frequently he or she who evaluates their performance and judges their eligibility for rehiring, for tenure, for pay increases, for new jobs.[29] The Teacher Center approach eliminates this risk, however, since teachers go to peers, not to the principal, for retraining opportunities. Collective bargaining also may have made it easier for teachers to admit a need for retraining, since matters of salary assignment and tenure are no longer solely associated with the principal's judgment.

10. Alternatives require curriculum development and new staffing patterns. Some alternative schools require that a curriculum be developed almost "from scratch," particularly in terms of instructional materials, diagnostics, and monitoring systems. For example, development of an integrated curriculum for open schools is just beginning, and there is a great deal of additional effort needed in this area. Other alternative programs require adaptation of existing materials.[30]

The original SEA approach to curriculum development involved a cadre of subject area consultants who were to serve all project schools. Unfortunately, this didn't work, so during the second project year some cadre members were assigned to a school where their skills and interests matched those of a particular alternative program. Others organized centers for curriculum development, such as an environmental science center to serve interested teachers. The contemporary school rejected the cadre altogether and contracted curriculum resource services from the University of Minnesota.

Curriculum change and the development of techniques for curriculum experimentation required increased opportunities for flexibility in staffing patterns. New techniques for legitimizing new staff/teacher roles, as well as procedures for retrenchment, were developed. Results were that each school was now able to employ parents in such jobs as teacher aide, visitor coordinator, volunteer coordinator, and that each school was allowed to redefine jobs in response to new needs.

(Teacher training institutions in colleges and universities should be much more alert than they have been to the responsibility of training teachers for new roles. Such a long-overdue response might significantly ease the financial and in-service development burdens now residing with local schools.)

A useful tool for both program and staff development was the project's internal evaluation program. A team of paid on-site evaluators (including parents) filled the need for immediate feedback as new ideas were tested in each school. Evaluators also examined areas of concern to all participants. They judged project plans and proposals, reviewed parent opinion surveys, studied characteristics of students drawn beyond neighborhood schools, conducted staff surveys, and reported findings to the management team. The dozens of reports produced by these internal evaluators provided detailed documentation of all major elements in the development of the SEA Project.[31]

11. Alternatives require efforts to harness the community's resources. SEA took a broad view of community resources, seeing them in terms of human,

material, and geographic possibilities, and developed mechanisms to tap all three
of them.[32]

SEA personnel developed new links with the University of Minnesota,
including joint faculty appointments, accommodations for pre-service intern
teachers, and the MPS/UM Teacher Center.

Parents and other community residents were in the schools daily — some as
paid staff, many as volunteers. Each SEA school hired a parent as a community
liaison to help parents with choice-making, to guide visitors, and to recruit
volunteers. In addition, some schools hired coordinators of volunteer services. In
the third project year, the two jobs were merged, and the position of community
resource coordinator was established.

The extent of volunteer service in the five SEA schools is impressive. A
survey made in 1974 shows that 200 volunteers (about half parents) worked for
1,400 hours in a typical week.[33]

12. The model project must be of manageable size. It must be large enough to
test the community's tolerance for a range of alternatives, large enough to involve
a representative sample of the district's students, large enough to be cost-effective.
It must be small enough, however, to operate without threatening the status quo
before it has proved itself.

In 1971, the SEA project involved 2,200 students in five schools, within a
school district of 65,000 students in 100 schools.

13. The model must be decently funded. Because SEA received $6.6 million
in federal funds over five years, observers have raised reasonable questions about
the financial ability of other districts to use the SEA model.

Several SEA participants, including the project business adviser, have argued
that "alternatives don't have to cost a lot more than existing programs; that what
must be done in a re-ordering of priorities for existing budget resources."[34]

In practice, however, this means competition for existing funds. The risk in
this approach is that it can make enemies who will be determined to "get" the
experimental program, and that this in turn may create undue pressure on everyone
in the program to get good evaluation results and to give the appearance of success,
rather than to provide a legitimate alternative for students and teachers.

A district which has successfully implemented a model project may be able to
broaden its base, without the need for large sums of additional money, by making
alternatives a major goal and by allocating existing staff development resources to
the program. (The growth of alternatives in Minneapolis, for example, from 2,200
students in SEA to more than 15,000 students systemwide over a four-year period
was funded primarily from the local operating budget after the School Board made
an alternative a major district goal.

But the model for alternatives — if it is to have any chance of success — must
begin with outside or uncommitted funds, or with a special appropriation from the
school board.

What, in fact, *do* alternatives cost?

- Available funds must be sufficient to bear the cost of renovating buildings
  and furniture to support different instructional arrangements. These are

one-time costs. (New buildings are not necessary; most SEA schools are fifty to sixty years old.)

- Funds for staff training are a must. The greater the departure the new programs make from previous programs, the greater the cost of retraining.

- Some additional staff will be required to meet new organizational and instructional needs: *i.e.*, curriculum resource help, community organizers, evaluation and dissemination services. (SEA had both internal and external evaluation services, a condition required by the federal grant.)

- Funds will be needed to purchase additional equipment and materials to provide instructions in new ways.[35]

- Transportation funds are another must, unless all the alternative programs are to be housed in a single building. It is meaningless to ask parents to consider sending children to a nonneighborhood school if they must provide daily transportation, particularly when elementary students are involved. (Both the alternatives and desegregation projects in Minneapolis have benefitted greatly from an eighty percent state reimbursement for student transportation costs.)

14. The model project must be given a chance to prove itself.

Time must be allowed for parent and community orientation, education, participation, and commitment; for developing and testing new curricula; for teachers to adapt to new places and to new methods; for gathering evaluation data on student achievement; for an effective governance structure to evolve.

Most government-funded innovative projects are three-year efforts. SEA's five-year time frame was unusual, and the planners' foresight was commendable. ESP required the school district to make a five-year commitment to comprehensive change and alternatives, and to report its progress toward these goals at regular intervals both to the federal government and to the community.

15. The model project will thrive with the aid of outside resources. External forces, pressures, and influences may not be essential to the success of the project, but they certainly help! Here is a brief list of such external aids.

- Many of the educational innovations tested by SEA came from the educational research and development laboratories located throughout the nation.

- SEA's federal grant provided both the impetus and the means for accomplishing public school change rapidly.

- The federal court became, in effect, the Minneapolis school district's ally by mandating (with only slight modifications) the desegregation program earlier adopted by the School Board.

- Strong support and encouragement also came from the Minnesota State Commissioner of Education and the State Department of Education which accepted the experimental program (the free school meets state graduation requirements).

- The Minnesota State Legislature's foundation aid approach to funding local schools, begun in 1971, took a large share of the burden of funding schools off local property taxpayers. The eighty percent reimbursement for transportation costs previously mentioned was an additional boost.

- The local news media set high standards for the public schools by continually "playing the theme" of moral and social responsibility. The objectivity and accuracy of their news stories aided change efforts, too. Good liaison with the media was a planned part of the Minneapolis effort.[36]

- The high expectations, encouragement, public statements, and financial support of Minneapolis businesses, industries, service groups, professions, and churches were powerful supports of the innovative programs. (The superintendent of schools was responsible for frequent and regular communication with the Chamber of Commerce, business, labor, civil, and church leaders.)

- Staff from the U.S. Office of Education, and later from the National Institute of Education, played a key role in SEA's development. From the moment the district learned of the ESP grant, people from Washington became interested, thoughtful visitors, evaluators, and participants in SEA. This gave the system the encouragement of an external force, and its administrators were moved to greater efforts by their desire to satisfy these outsiders. It wasn't the same as one assistant superintendent helping the other, it was more than that. Each time visitors came, there was a flow of adrenalin and an ego involvement among staff to prove that it could do what it had said it would get done.

- Finally, in an incomplete list, there was the climate of the time. Respect and acceptance of human differences which grew out of the civil rights movement of the 50's and 60's resulted in new levels of tolerance for people, ideas, and programs that differed from traditional ones. There was a surge of hope and a new search for ways to improve the human condition, including a willingness to consider changes in the pattern of the public schools.

SUMMARY: FROM MODEL TO MAINSTREAM

At the outset, the plan was to begin SEA in a relatively secluded and independent environment. Gradually, new programs and strategies proved effective were to be 'exported' to other city schools. Finally, the project schools were to return as an integral part of the school system.[37]

In short, the challenge was to get something going, to prove it, to use it, and then to bring it into the mainstream as quickly as possible. That process is underway in Minneapolis, and the alternative option has been exercised by sixty percent of the city's elementary students.

SEA's overriding impact on the school district was to open minds to change. In so doing, it has allowed an extending of the bounds beyond tradition, and provided the base for a comparative analysis, so the dsitrict could make some valid judgments from among several educational models.[38]

The effect of SEA was to create a citywide yearning for alternatives and to produce a healthy competition among schools. The demand came from parents of various economic, cultural, and racial backgrounds. Fortunately, there were school people within the system willing to be their advocates and a School Board which was determined to provide sound educational alternatives to all who wanted them.

Another, even longer chapter could have been written on how the number of students in alternative programs grew from SEA's 2,200 to more than 15,000 — sixty percent of the elementary students in the whole city — in just four years. Certainly, one critical event in this development was School Board action making alternatives a major goal of the school district, and setting a time line for implementation. The need to desegregate the schools was another major catalyst for quick implementation, as was the construction of four large elementary schools serving 500 to 1,800 students. Each school now provides space and facilities for alternative programs, and the two largest house traditional, continuous progress, and open programs.

Other strategies and circumstances included the following: the administrative decision to devote a large share of local staff development funds to training for alternatives; School Board and administration willingness to share the governance function with parents and teachers; the accessibility of SEA model schools as training grounds where teachers and principals could and did serve internships; use of the Teacher Center approach to staff training; and exportation of SEA administrators to key positions in other school district areas.

Momentum for alternatives was accelerated further by evaluation results which showed that children in SEA alternative schools did at least as well as children in traditional schools. SEA's high student retention rates also contributed to this momentum. While citywide K-12 enrollment declined between the fall of 1971 and the fall of 1976, from 65,000 to 52,500 students, SEA enrollment increased during the same period from 2,200 to 2,263 students.

Larry Reynolds points out that ''SEA was on the cutting edge of educational thought and practice.''[39] Yet, in five brief years — not the twenty to thirty years that research has indicated are necessary for such change — many SEA innovations became part of the mainstream of the educational effort in Minneapolis. There are many, many students, parents, teachers, and principals today who believe that public education in Minneapolis is better, more responsive, and more productive for an infinite variety of students who present themselves for education than it was before the advent of the alternatives.[40]

Magnet Schools: From Students' and Parents' Perspectives

5

Magnet Schools: From Students' and Parents' Perspectives

GAIL GRAFFLIN FULLINGTON

Introduction

In this chapter, Gail Fullington reports directly on some of the views held by students who attend Dallas Magnets. The actual quotations grew out of visits to Magnet Schools and through conversations there with students and parents.

The history of education in America has been marked by a continual redefinition in response to societal demands. Several such redefinitions have occurred in this decade alone, among them the one growing out of the recent emphasis on Magnet Schools. Considerable research on student learning has indicated that, contrary to earlier belief, there is no "one best system" that enables students to learn or teachers to teach (Tyack, 1974). In fact it is increasingly evident that persistent reassertion of "the one best system" simply will not do (Sizer, 1976). Students clearly learn equally well in a variety of ways in a variety of settings *OSSC,* 1974).

This fact, together with the increasingly complex demands of society, has made it imperative for education to become a process of matching parents' demands and students' learning styles with schooling structures (or alternatives) that meet these demands and styles. The time is near when educators will be concerned with operating a kind of "brokerage service" or "consumer guide" whose purpose will be to assist students and parents in selecting educational alternatives that will best meet their needs. As a matter of fact, many districts already offer such services, among them such diverse systems as the ones in Eugene, Oregon, and Cincinnati, Ohio.

A *Magnet* School is one kind of alternative program oriented toward specific interest area *(OSSC).* The term "Magnet School" means "a school or education center that offers a special curriculum capable of attracting substantial numbers of students of different racial backgrounds" *(Education USA,* 1976).* Magnets are developed according to a "center of excellence" concept that combines basic academic programs with a specialty enrichment program (Brandstetter and Foster, 1976). Each Magnet offering is intended to be unique, and it is that uniqueness which is able, ideally, to attract students from across school boundary lines, and to blend economic classes and races while it meets the varied needs of the students who choose to attend. More than anything else, it is this potential for blending races and economic levels that has made the Magnet School so appealing to urban districts dissatisfied with busing as a means of achieving racial balance.

*Though the author recognizes that Magnet Schools can exist at all grade levels, for the purposes of this study the term "Magnet School" will refer to a secondary school.

Historical Precedents for Magnet Schools

The Magnet School concept is not a new one. Historically, parents and students, as well as professional educators, have sought choices *outside* those offered by traditional schools — choices that allow for developing "specific interest areas" among students, choices that meet a variety of society's needs. As early as the mid-1800's, reaction to the Boston Latin Grammar School's rather narrow and elitist curriculum led to demands for more accessible high schools. Originally created to prepare boys for Harvard, the school's purpose was to produce an elite clergy. Clearly, it was not meant for everyone, nor was there any other place to go for those not allowed to attend it (Elliott, 1905).

Dissatisfaction with the school's admissions policies led to the Academy Movement of the mid-1800's, an attempt to counter its "limited curriculum and exclusively college-preparatory ends," which were viewed as "wholly inadequate for the needs of the youth of the land" (Cubberley, 1919). Disillusionment with the uniformity of the Academy curriculum, however, soon resulted in the creation of differentiated programs within existing high schools, as well as in separately established ones. It was this differentiation that established the precedent for today's Magnet Schools. Cubberley notes that, after 1880, several new subjects and parallel four-year courses were introduced into the high schools. Though the curriculum included the classical courses offered before, it added such "innovations [as the] scientific course, the business course, the manual arts course," etc. These were not simply separate classes which students could choose to attend and then blend into the total student body for what we now call "core curriculum" classes. These were separate, tracked courses of study in specific interest areas which kept students separated throughout the school day.

Perhaps more easily identifiable precedents for the Magnet School were the manual arts/industrial training schools of the late 1800's and early 1900's. Rapidly growing industrialization raised questions about the high school's capacity to prepare students for industrial careers, and these led in turn to demands for business and manual training. This concern is clearly expressed in the following citation: "For the most part . . . high schools were not providing technical skills for industry and commerce; in fact, they were accused by critics of being hopelessly out of joint with the times in that they provided allegedly useless studies" (Krug, 1964).

Butler's *Educational Review* hailed the manual arts movement as a "forward step," proclaiming that manual training was most successful when "isolated in a building specially prepared for the purpose" and "conducted by specially trained teachers'' (Krug). While critics of the movement, like Dean E.A. Birge of the University of Wisconsin, argued that separate schools were undemocratic and "distinctly for the working people," the stage was clearly set for the creation of special purpose schools separate from the regular, or more traditional, high schools. Although the manual training movement continued, it was overshadowed in the early 1900's by a movement for increased industrial/vocational training.

With schools like the Skyline Career Development Center in Dallas and the Philadelphia Parkway Program, the movement to vocational training (within a specialized setting and with specially trained teachers where students could choose to attend from across school boundary lines) reached its peak in the late 1960's and early 1970's. Skyline, with its specialized, highly sophisticated curriculum and facility offerings, attracted students to its career clusters from every high school attendance area in the Dallas Independent School District. The offerings ranged from aeronautics (complete with hangar and planes) to television (complete with studio and closed-circuit broadcast facilities).

What the early academies, manual training courses, industrial/vocational education, and the Skyline and Parkway programs all have in common with today's Magnet Schools is that they represent interest area choices for parents and students well beyond what is offered in the "traditional" high school curriculum. In short, they offer "alternatives" that attract students on the basis of interest in some specialized programs rather than on the basis of residence in a particular school attendance area.

Magnet Schools and Desegregation

Since the *Brown v. Board of Education* decisions in 1954 and 1955, school districts have sought viable means for achieving desegregation. Particularly, the city school systems have been seeking alternatives to busing, prevalent since *Swann v. Charlotte-Mecklenburg* in 1971. Magnet Schools may provide part of the answer to this problem. By offering a specialized and unique curriculum, it is hoped that Magnet Schools will attract students of all races and economic levels on a voluntary basis, thus making busing as the sole means for achieving racial balance unnecessary.

In Dallas, Houston, and other large cities, Magnet Schools are a part of court-adopted desegregation orders, indicating that both the courts and the cities involved believe that these schools can become a means for voluntary desegregation. Increasingly, too, statements of national educational policy focus on Magnet Schools as an alternative to busing.

Mario Fantini believes that "the courts are accepting Magnet School programs because judges feel that specialized schools offering concentrated curricula . . . will draw a racially and economically mixed student body without having to mandate busing" *(Education USA)*. A provision of the Emergency School Aid Act calls for the spending of $25 million in 1977 and $50 million in 1978 for planning and operating Magnet Schools and "neutral site" schools, and for pairing schools with colleges or business concerns.

In *Tasby v. Estes* (1976), Judge William M. Taylor, Jr. stated that "The most realistic, feasible, and effective method for eliminatig remaining vestiges of a dual system on the 9-12 level, and for providing equal educational opportunity without regard to race, is the institution of magnet schools throughout the DISD (Dallas Independent School District).

That national interest in Magnet Schools is increasing is further evidenced by growing ESAA funding, congressional interest, and other support at the national policy-making level. The 1976 Democratic Party Platform, for example, contains a statement of "support for incentive programs to achieve integrated education — among them, the Magnet School concept." The Council of the Great City Schools, an organization of twenty-eight of the country's largest urban districts, adopted as a part of its 1976 policy platform a statement favoring "federal and state incentives for developing creative approaches to desegregation and integration, such as magnet and specialty schools."

Whether the Magnet School will prove to be the solution to school desegregation that its proponents hope is not yet known. Certainly, there is room for other creative, viable solutions to the desegregation dilemma, and, just as clearly, such solutions have not yet been found. Perhaps the Magnet School concept will ultimately prove to be one kind of solution.

As important as the Magnet School's function in desegregation appears to be, that function can be successful only insofar as the major function of the school itself is successful: *i.e.*, providing unique, specialized curriculum choices in special interest areas for students. Unless students choose to attend, Magnet Schools will clearly not succeed.

Magnet Schools as Alternatives

The number of alternative school programs in America has grown dramatically. A recent (1973) estimate puts the total figure "for alternative elementary and secondary schools at more that 3,000, and one projection indicates that there will be close to 20,000 such schools in operation by 1976" (NASSP, 1973). Reasons for this rapid growth are varied. At least one group of researchers feels that the major reason is the element of choice that alternative education offers the community. Parents and students tend to be more loyal and committed to schools they choose; similarly, teachers are happier with students who are in their classes by choice. "This open market creates a healthy feedback from the consumer to the professional educator" (Smith, Burke, and Barr, 1975). Because of this feedback, alternative schools are more responsive to community needs, and so receive greater community support.

Dunn and Dunn (1974) argue that, while student choice is important, educators must make more of an effort to assist in "matching" the learning situation with the learner so that there is a maximum "fit" between the student's learning style and the learning setting.

In the progress of alternative education, normal educational goals are by no means either subverted or abandoned. On the contrary, "alternative public education means diversifying the means to common ends" (Fantini, 1973).

In another context, Fantini has gone on to point out that "The system of public schools of choice...assumes that the parties closest to the action — parents and students as consumers, and teachers and administrators as professionals — should have the right to make choices from legitimate alternatives" (Fantini, 1970).

Alternative schools — including Magnet Schools — give students *and* their parents choice in the kinds of curriculum, settings, and teaching in which they would like to participate. Indeed, the success of Magnet Schools depends on their ability not only to provide choices that are attractive, but also to assist students and parents in making those choices. Abramson (1975) states that the goal of educational alternatives is "to match child, material and methodology on an individualized basis." He argues that truly student-centered education is best reached through alternatives. "If education is to be centered on something, it must be centered on the child, not the method."

In describing Philadelphia's Parkway Program, which began in 1969 and which has served as a model for change in secondary education ever since, Finkelstein (1976) states that initially the program was:

> ...determined to show that...while traditional schools were valid and working for many students, these schools did not provide sufficient options for an increasing number of turned-off, tuned-out young people.

Chase and Buchanan (1977) report that:

> ...a number of students, who have not previously enjoyed much academic success, are finding themselves in the new environments [Magnet Schools] and developing stronger self-concepts...[a] number of these students...now exhibit high capabilities for leadership and a will to overcome deficiencies in learning skills.

But alternatives and Magnets are not just for "turned-off, tuned-out" young people. According to Fantini (1970):

> The aim of participation in our society is to promote individual choice. In an open society that values the individual, making choices from among various options of public education ought to be the right of every individual.

Fantini further asserts that public education can no longer be viewed as the kind of "one best system" that Tyack describes. Instead, it provides a range of options for a diverse population, with numerous means to achieve common goals.

> The standard school is certainly one alternative to quality education. However, it is no longer a suitable alternative for growing numbers of teachers, parents and students who need different kinds of programs now.

Previously, the student knew "that there *was* only one path — and he must either accept it and adjust to it or perish." Today, Fantini concludes, it is recognized that there are many paths, and that students and their parents can choose from among them.

In their study of Magnet Schools, Chase and Buchanan (1977) report high student morale in most curriculum areas. Because they've made free choices, the students feel motivated and responsible for their choices and respond with commitment to the school and its goals. In one Magnet School, for example, "expensive equipment is left unguarded, but vandalism and theft have not resulted. The sense of community and a common value system have established pride in the school and a belief in its objectives."

It is the element of choice, then, that holds the answer to the success or failure of Magnet Schools. As alternatives, they must offer the specific interest areas that most attract students. Even more, unless these interest areas attract students of diverse ethnic and economic levels, the entire usefulness of the Magnet School concept in terms of the voluntary desegregation and integration of urban school districts can be threatened.

Why Students Choose Magnet Schools: Four Case Studies

Why *do* students leave their home schools and neighborhoods to travel, sometimes several miles, and by choice, to a Magnet School? What do they find when they get there? Do their parents support this choice?

This study does not claim to have statistically quantifiable data to answer these questions fully. What it does present in the case histories which follow are student and parent answers to the questions — and *in their own words*. To secure material for the case histories, the author visited the Magnet Schools in Dallas, Texas, and interviewed both students and parents in order to gain as broad an overview as possible of their reactions and feelings.

CASE 1: CARLA

Carla is sixteen. She was a sophomore last year in her home high school. Bright, articulate, and outgoing, Carla has always been interested in science. At her home high school, she completed the only chemistry and biology courses that were offered there. Since then, she has decided that she wants a career in medicine, although just what that career will be she isn't sure yet.

Carla's parents share her enthusiasm for her career choice, but they couldn't afford to pay for the tutoring or private school courses she might well need to have at this point. For Carla and her parents, the Health Professions Center (one of Dallas' Magnet Schools), seemed the answer.

Having enrolled as a part-time student in the fall of 1976, Carla now plans to become a full-time student in the Health Professions Center.

Why?

"My teachers at the other school were good, and they taught me a lot," Carla feels, "but my teachers here are real doctors and nurses, and I get to work in a real hospital with real patients. My old biology classroom can't beat that!''

Many of Carla's medical preparatory courses *are* taught by licensed physicians, nurses, and other professionals in a facility that provides modern, professional laboratories and equipment. Since the Health Professions Center is located adjacent to Baylor Hospital, it is easy for Carla to enrich her classroom learning by volunteering for hospital duty two afternoons a week after school. Next year, she hopes to work part-time at Baylor (after school and on weekends) in hopes of gaining valuable, on-the-job experience to supplement her studies, as well as of earning money for college or medical school.

While Carla and her parents feel that it is still too early for her to identify a particular career within medicine, they are confident the experience she is now gaining will help her make a more intelligent choice later. "She's getting so much experience in so many fields," says her mother, "that it is giving her a chance to look at those fields first-hand, so that when it's time for her to decide what she really wants to do, she'll know — she won't have to guess whether it's what she wants, and find out too late that it isn't."

Has she missed her friends and the life of her old high school? "Yes, I miss some of my friends," Carla admits. "But I still see them when I'm back at my other school the rest of the day. And next year, when I'm here full time, I'll still see them after school and on weekends. Besides, some of my friends have decided that they'll try the Magnet School next year, since I like it so well. And I've made new friends, too, that have the same interests as I do."

These interests include preparatory training in several medical careers — office personnel, practicing medicine, medical technology, physical therapy, pharmacy, nursing, X-ray technology, and veterinary medicine. They also include dentistry — *e.g.*, dental hygiene, oral surgery, and dental technology.

Carla's friends in other programs, like Carla herself, are instructed by licensed physicians, dentists, technologists, nurses, and other professionals. The courses are conducted in modern, professionally equipped laboratories where there is the opportunity to observe and work in real-life clinical settings under the supervision of expert instructors. Some of the top medical personnel in the city serve on the advisory committee of the center, supervising the curriculum and the students' work experiences. And, when Carla and her friends are ready for jobs or for more advanced training, the skills they've learned at the Health Professions Center will make them highly employable and excellent candidates for the country's top pre-medical and pre-dental schools.

Would she choose the Health Professions Center if she had the choice to make all over again?

"Sure, I would," answers Carla; "only sooner."

CASES 2 AND 3: TONY AND ANDREA

Tony is seventeen, and a junior. He's been interested in music "for as long as I can remember," and played trumpet in the band at his home high school. Although his academic grades are not spectacular ("I'd rather get with some of my

friends and jam for a couple of hours than study, any day!'' he admits), Tony
manages nonetheless to maintain average grades.

Jazz is Tony's special interest, and he can tell you about every great jazz
musician who ever lived. His ambition is one day to play professionally in a jazz
group. His instructors at the Creative Arts Academy, another of the Dallas Magnet
Schools, feel that he not only has the talent but the determination, as well, to
realize his career goal.

''Oh, I'd played in the band in my old school, but I'd done about all I could do
there. Besides, a lot of the other kids looked at me like I was crazy when I said I
wanted to play jazz — they're only into rock. And I like rock, too, but jazz is what I
really like!'' Tony says.

It was with reluctance that Tony's parents agreed to allow him to transfer to
the Magnet School. ''He was so involved at his old school, with the band there and
all, that we were afraid he wouldn't be happy, that he'd miss all the activity he was
used to,'' says Tony's dad.

''Sure, I miss all that,'' responds Tony, ''but one of my teachers from the
other school came here to teach and I've made several new friends. It was worth
it.''

Tony's program includes not only intensive training on his chosen instru-
ment, but also advanced instruction in composition, interpretation, improvisation,
arranging, and conducting. As a member of the performing jazz ensemble at the
Magnet School, Tony has the opportunity to perform publicly in the kind of group
he would want to belong to some day as a professional.

In addition to music, Tony's classmates at the Creative Arts Academy receive
intensive instruction from professionals in the performing and visual arts in such
areas as dance, theater, sculpture, painting, weaving, jewelry design, etc.

Housed in one of the city's oldest school buildings, the Creative Arts
Academy is able to make unique use of the full proscenium, the huge backstage
area, the courtyard, and the high ceilings and wide hallways so characteristic of old
buildings. Broad, winding stairways have become canvases for murals created and
designed by students; the high-ceilinged and windowed third-floor room that once
housed the study hall has become a ballet studio; wide sections of hallway have
become open-area sketch workshops; the large and open courtyard, an outdoor
theater. The building's transformation from a drab, old building into a unique arts
facility is itself a tribute to the talents of the established artists who teach there as
well as the budding artists who study there.

Walking through the dance classrooms is like walking through the quarters of
a professional repertory company. One sees intense young men and women
working with professional ballet and modern dance teachers in professionally
equipped rehearsal and performance halls as they learn the rudiments of time,
shape, color, and rhythm.

In addition to the dance and music programs, the theater arts program gives
students a chance to study all aspects of the theater: acting, scenery construction,
set design, makeup, sound, lighting, costume design and construction. All
productions at the Academy — instrumental music, dance, theater, or vocal music

— are produced by students who use their training to handle production details, as well as to direct and design the productions on occasion. In the process, the young artists learn to respect and appreciate each other's talents.

Andrea, one of Tony's classmates at the Academy, is a sophomore; but, unlike Tony, she is enrolled in the visual arts program. Her special interest is sculpture. "I've always been interested in art," she says, "and it seems like I've been fooling around with clay for as long as I can remember."

Andrea had planned to attend Dallas' Skyline Career Development Center, but when she heard about the Creative Arts Academy she decided to give it a try, instead. "These Magnet Schools are the best thing Dallas has come up with," she feels. Although she does express some concerns about the academic program, Andrea remains enthusiastic about her experiences at the Academy. "They really let you do what you're interested in, and try it out. In a normal art course, you don't get to try very much — I mean, in sculpture, you get a little lump of clay and you maybe make a figure or a pinch pot or something. They just can't offer anything like this."

For Andrea, "this" means intensive training in form, color, composition, and abstraction, plus expression in various other visual media so that she can learn to understand the interrelationships among the different media at the same time she is concentrating on her own.

As do other Magnet Schools in Dallas, the Creative Arts Academy utilizes the expertise of professionals from the community who advise, teach, demonstrate, and critique — as well as employ — the young artists who study there.

Careers open to graduates of the Academy include composing, conducting, performing, clothing design and marketing, sculpture, jewelry design, jewelry making and marketing, printmaking, and pottery.

"The teachers here have a more personal relationship with students," Tony feels. "It's like we're equal, like we're all performers, you know? I like that."

Apparently, the other students also "like that." The Academy is Dallas' most successful Magnet School, with over 300 full-time and 760 part-time students who, like Andrea and Tony, have found a way to continue their academic educations while enhancing their talents and preparing for artistic careers.

CASE 4: KATHY

Kathy looks more like a recently employed high school graduate than a student in her junior year. She currently attends the Business and Management Center, another of the Magnet Schools in the Dallas Independent School District. Though previously enrolled in a secretarial course in her old high school, Kathy chose to transfer to the Business and Management Center for several reasons. For one, she thinks that after graduation she'll have a better chance to land the kind of job she wants as a legal secretary. "Eventually, I might want to go to law school, but I don't know yet," she says.

The Business and Management Center is located in the oldest high school building in Dallas. The school, which was once some distance from the central business district, is now situated on prime downtown property, thus enabling its students to work part-time in real office settings. Furthermore, its proximity to the business heart of the city allows industrial and professional leaders to participate more easily in the program and to be valuable additions to the regular staff.

Kathy's classmates are training for such careers as business management, marketing, insurance, real estate, investment, accounting, computer science, merchandising, and clerical work.

Problems Facing Magnet Schools

In spite of the good beginnings they have made and their enthusiastic reception by students and parents, Magnet Schools still face two crucial problems: finance and certification. The cost involved in establishing a Magnet School program prohibits many school districts from doing so — districts, in fact, which both critically need and desire such programs. The Emergency School Aid Act has appropriated $25 million in 1977 for Magnet Schools, an amount which, though not sufficient to meet program needs, does represent the beginning of significant federal support for Magnet Schools. But other solutions which will allow Magnet Schools either to pay for themselves or to receive vastly increased federal funding must be sought.

Certification rules in many states prohibit the use of state funds for the salaries of professionals who are not certified as teachers. Alternatives to present certification requirements must be developed which will allow the salaries of non-certified professionals who teach in Magnet Schools to be paid with state funds, rather than exclusively with local funds.

Magnet Schools clearly are not for everyone, just as their more traditional counterparts are not for everyone. However, they *are* for the student who has identified and seriously wishes to pursue a particular talent or career interest in a setting which allows his or her uniqueness to be more fully nurtured.

What Carla, Tony, Andrea, and Kathy have in common with other students in Dallas' Magnet high schools is that they are studying in just such settings. And while these may resemble traditional secondary schools from the outside, inside the buildings one finds facilities, equipment, personnel, and opportunities that could never be found elsewhere. By choosing these opportunities, Carla, Tony, Andrea, and Kathy have voluntarily desegregated their city's schools — even though they did not consciously do so.

In any case they, their parents, and their city very much like what they've found.

Alternative Schools:
Program Marketing and Student Recruitment

or

How to Sell Alternative Schools
to Kids and Families

6

Alternative Schools:
Program Marketing and Student Recruitment

or

How to Sell Alternative Schools
to Kids and Families

DONALD R. WALDRIP and EDGAR J. LOTSPEICH

Introduction

The authors, Donald R. Waldrip and Edgar J. Lotspeich, explain how to encourage students to attend alternatives. The job, they say, must not be left to chance and cannot be done by a public relations firm. A public relations firm might generate a general *recruitment effort; but the* focused *effort–getting certain students to explore the possibilities of attending alternatives–should be conducted primarily by persons with experience in the field of education: consultants, teachers, and other educational staff.*

Background

School districts have always faced the challenge of "how best to serve a captive audience." Legally enforceable compulsory attendance has been a mainstay of the American experience and, indeed, the ultimate responsibility for assuring attendance resides beyond the schools themselves—with our juvenile justice system.

Student enrollment has been a "given" for public education, and its yearly fluctuation within a district is a function of such external variables as birth rates, shifts in populations, and competition from private and parochial schools—to say nothing of the local billiards establishment and the nearest fishing hole. School-aged children residing within the district who do not attend private or parochial schools define the enrolled population which the district must serve. Geographic attendance areas have determined who will attend what school, and the establishment of a common curriculum has guaranteed equality of educational opportunity within communities.

Since parents, once having established their place of residence, are generally unable to select the public school their children will attend, boards of education have attempted to ensure that the quality of education they receive is equal—not necessarily good, but equal—no matter what school in the district they go to. Equality of educational opportunity has therefore found expression in common curriculum and instructional methods and, within each district, in a constant (general-fund supported) per capita expenditure.

For years educators have disagreed—sometimes loudly, almost always persuasively—about the best method of educating youngsters. They have also argued about *what* should be taught and, within the context of the traditional grade structure, *when*. In fact, many—including the authors—have spent a great amount of time attempting to eliminate such traditional structures.

We all remember the days when "progressive" educators advocated modular scheduling, team teaching, and continuous progress education in the ungraded school. There is no doubt that advocates of these methodologies contributed greatly to the re-examination of our conventional lock-step educational system, and that they were absolutely right in their conclusions—at least insofar as a great number of students were concerned. Many children, of course, function better in more open-ended, flexible settings, but even these do not serve *all* students well.

The admission that there is no *one* best method for educating *all* children— one of the most important admissions in the history of education—was the beginning of the alternative school movement. For years it has been clear that children have different needs, aspirations, and even learning styles; but, until the advent of the Magnet School, educators somehow expected all of these differences to be addressed by a single classroom teacher or, at best, a "team" of two or three teachers.

The establishment of alternative education—with schools and programs that parents and children could voluntarily select, with diverse curriculum and instructional methods—requires a re-orientation by the district to its parent/student constituency. In fact, in one instance, the commitment to re-define the traditional relationship between a school district and its parent/student constituency (Alum Rock's NIE-sponsored Voucher System) led directly to the establishment of alternative schools.

The basis of this new relationship is best expressed by two interdependent elements: *choice* and *options*. Alternative education, in whatever form it assumes, must allow for real parent/student choice through the creation of a number of educational options from which parents and students can freely select. Program marketing and student recruitment are the processes of developing these options and encouraging voluntary student enrollment in the option each student elects. An effective program marketing and student recruitment strategy incorporates all the decisions and activities which result in parents' and/or students' selecting programs which are uniquely different from the ones to which, under a conventional system, they would be assigned. Such steps, however, are foreign to most school districts (which have always been assured of their captive audience) and therefore constitute a subject about which much confusion remains.

SOME USEFUL DEFINITIONS

Program marketing—or the marketing of alternative schools—includes decisions which determine the kinds of alternatives to be offered, the grade levels to be served, and the school sites to be selected. Marketing also concerns decisions about student transportation, student eligibility and entrance requirements (if any), and the possible relationships among the alternatives offered. Program marketing, of course, precedes sales (student recruitment) and so determines the attractiveness of the alternatives.

Student recruitment, on the other hand, includes all actions designed to generate applications for admission to alternative schools. This is the direct sales effort, and selling alternative schools—like selling any product—relies heavily upon getting information out through various means.

Sales campaigns can be either *general* or *focused*. Heavy reliance upon mass media—newspaper inserts, radio and television public service announcements (PSA's), and brochures that are either distributed to students throughout the school district or else mailed directly to parents—constitutes what one may call a *general* student recruitment campaign. Direct and personal channels of communication— *e.g.*, letters of recommendation, phone banks, community meetings, and parent/ student conferences with program staff—go into making up a *focused* student recruitment campaign. A successful recruitment effort will tend to incorporate both general and focused campaigns. Of course, the type of communication mix and the effort expended will be determined by *how much* the school district wants to reach *how many* students and parents.

Commitment and Specific Objectives

Before a school district can formally initiate a marketing and recruitment process, it must define for itself its level of commitment to alternative education as well as its specific objectives. Since the move to alternative schools requires that the system undertake a fundamentally unique direction, it must have a good idea of just what it is seeking to accomplish, and the extent to which it is willing—and able—to support alternative programs. A parent's willingness to enroll his or her children in alternative schools signifies a long-term commitment to this kind of schooling. This is a big decision for a parent, and it must be responsibly reciprocated by the district itself—even though alternative education, like all education today, is susceptible to the often unpredictable dynamics of the market place and the whims of politicians. Alternative schools, for example, can be equally threatened by lack of interest—which results in small enrollments in programs, thus making them difficult to justify on the basis of cost—or by excessive interest, which results in large numbers of student applications, many of which will have to be rejected because of oversubscription. Ideally, a district's commitment will develop and sustain alternatives in proportion to the willingness, at any point, of its student/parent constituency to participate in the school options being offered.

Examples of specific needs which can best be served by alternative education include:

1. *the need to reduce racial isolation within the school system by voluntary means*

2. *the need to retain a middle-income constituency, both white and black, in the school system*

3. *the need to respond creatively to identifiable interest groups seeking changes within the system that other groups may oppose*

4. *the need to provide unique curriculum content and alternative instructional methods*

5. *the need to involve and benefit from the special resources and skills of major institutions–both public and private–thereby gaining their support for public education.*

Obviously, a district's level of commitment to alternative education, and the number of specific objectives it attempts to satisfy, will determine the character and scope of the marketing and recruitment process. For instance, a school system seeking to involve other institutions is well advised to place an emphasis upon content-oriented programs (such as an environmental learning center or a school for the creative and performing arts) whose content makes working arrangements with outside institutions possible and desirable. Programs stressing unique instructional methods often fail to provide any basis for such external linkages.

In Dallas, for example, many businesses have "adopted" certain schools. Representatives of a business will participate in "selling" the Magnet School to the community, and the students of that Magnet will subsequently have an opportunity to learn how that business operates. In St. Louis, Monsanto and the Washington University Medical School held a joint press conference to tell the city how these two organizations would work actively in the instructional program of an elementary alternative school which was located in the inner-city and emphasized scientific exploration and experimentation. After the media carried a story of how professionals from Monsanto and the Medical School would help teach certain classes, and how the laboratories of the two institutions would be used for actual classroom experiences, the alternative school received more applications than it could handle. The same relationship was established between Mallenkrodt and the Math-Science High School, between two arts Magnets and the most prestigious cultural and artistic organizations in St. Louis, and, finally, between a career-oriented elementary school and the Ralston-Purina Company. None of these linkages could have been forged if the unique characteristics of the programs had been structural (e.g., open school, IGE, etc.) in nature. (Alternatives based on structural differences such as those offered in Minneapolis can be effective, however, from the standpoint of improved instructional offerings or of the reduction of racial isolation.)

Developing alternatives in a manner which guarantees a reduction in racial isolation through voluntary means will also have impact on program marketing and student recruitment—particularly, in determining the locations of the schools. But marketing and recruitment, in the absence of a specified level of commitment and clearly stated objectives is, at best, a frustrating enterprise and one that is subject to constant turmoil and conflict. In those instances where alternative education has proved to be less than successful, the cause can be traced either to the absence of any real commitment and/or well-defined and practical objectives, or to a program marketing and student recruitment effort which was conducted independently of these considerations.

Program Marketing

A. KINDS OF ALTERNATIVES AND SITE SELECTIONS

The kind of alternative desired will quite often dictate the site at which it can be located. Since the reduction of racial isolation through voluntary means has served as a major objective for alternative education in many school systems, special emphasis should be placed on this objective in any discussion of site selection.

1. *Neutral-Site Alternative or Magnet School*

   a. *Definition:* A neutral-site alternative or Magnet School is a free-standing, self-contained program designed to serve students at specified grade levels throughout the district on a first-come, first-served basis consistent with attaining a racially balanced student enrollment. With the exception of a college preparatory school, or an accelerated school, neutral-site Magnets do not have entrance requirements *per se* —though teacher recommendations and interviews may be used in screening applicants for interest, aptitude, or aspiration. No student is automatically given a "prior right" to attend a neutral-site school because he or she was enrolled at the site where the alternative is being implemented. Ideally, a neutral-site school's student body and faculty will constitute a community of interests that is given definition by the prevailing theme or unique focus of the curriculum. Neutral-site schools are usually content-oriented; that is, they exist to serve students who desire to pursue a unique, but broadly defined curriculum. (This, however, is not always the case; consider some of the fundamental alternatives springing up across the country.) Specific examples of neutral-site, content-oriented schools are: a school for the creative and performing arts, a school for the humanities, a college prep school, a school for mathematics and science, and a school for law and government.

   b. *Site Selection:* Since neutral-site schools are intended to be free-standing and self-contained, they are usually based in a facility which is given over totally to the resident alternative program. This facility will serve no other student population than that enrolled in the alternative. Leased facilities and/or school buildings vacated by prior board action are usually sought for neutral-site schools. When necessary the school can share a facility with a regular student body, but *only* if the two schools can coexist as essentially independent entities sharing common facilities.

Since most school systems have a total student enrollment (market) to fill only one of each kind of alternative school, these schools should be centrally located within the district or subdistrict. This provides equal access for all students. It is equally important, however, that alternative schools with an instructional program dependent upon association with external institutions be located reasonably close to those institutions. Previous experience suggests that it is possible, though difficult admittedly, to recruit racially balanced entry grade levels (e.g., ninth and tenth graders for a school slated to become a nine-to-twelve program) at sites located in low-income, predominantly minority communities. Higher income, predominantly white communities are usually not centrally located enough to permit their consideration as sites for one-of-a-kind, neutral-site schools. Sites within "middle city," racially mixed, and institution-dominated communities (e.g., a university or medical center setting) often allow for maximum recruitment.

If a neutral-site school should become oversubscribed, thereby requiring a change of site (even if the new site is viewed as less attractive), happy and productive children of supportive parents will usually elect to follow the school to the new site. Location directly influences the numbers of applications to a school, but it apparently becomes a secondary matter once a student has become involved with the program itself. For example, the Creative and Performing Arts School of Cincinnati has moved three times in its four years of existence. It opened as a grade four-to-six school in a 106-year-old building located in an "arty" area of the city. The second year, a new fourth grade arrived, making the school a grade four-to-seven school, whereupon the school expanded into halls, into the community center, and into a room above Mike's Meat Market across the street. Dedicated violin students often practiced their pizzicatos in an empty washroom. The third year, as more children and grades were added, the school moved into two rented facilities, three blocks from each other. Finally, in the fourth year, the school, now known as SCPA—say that slowly—and serving grades four-to-ten, moved into a very old, very large secondary structure located downtown in what had been considered an unacceptable location only four years earlier. Interestingly enough, virtually all the students followed the school through its moves and evolution.

2. *Neighborhood Magnet School*

a. *Definition:* Neighborhood Magnet Schools, like neutral-site alternative schools, are free-standing, self-contained, educational programs. Unlike neutral-site schools, however, they exist primarily to serve a student population already enrolled in a neighborhood school which has been converted into a Magnet. Previously enrolled students are usually given a prior right of attendance, after which "district-wide students" are admitted on a first-come, first-served basis (so long as this is consistent with achieving a racially balanced student body, and does not exceed the capacity of the school). Since neighborhood Magnets primarily serve pre-existing student bodies, they tend to place emphasis upon a unique instructional method. Examples of neighborhood Magnets are IGE schools, Career Awareness Centers, and Action Learning Centers. Neighborhood Magnets also tend to place a greater emphasis on *how* a student learns, while neutral-site schools usually stress instructional *content*. Even though this distinction often becomes blurred (because of variance in local definitions), from the standpoint of program marketing and student recruitment the distinction is quite clear.

Neutral-site, district-wide schools will attract more students if they have a specific subject-matter emphasis. For example, a performing arts school will attract more students than will an IGE school, but it is easier (and, ultimately, more productive) to convince a neighborhood school with excess capacity to become an "open" school or an IGE school than to become a math-science center, for example. Strangely, the one exception appears to be the fundamental school, which tends to operate better at a neutral site. Rarely can parents from an entire attendance area decide to allow "their" school to convert to the fundamental model; a small number of dissidents seem always to emerge.

b. *Site Selection Criteria:* The most obvious site selection criterion for a neighborhood Magnet is that it be set up at a school which has ample excess capacity. Magnets implemented at schools already near capacity will result in the denial of admission to the vast majority of district-wide student applicants. Unfortunately, such Magnets do exist and, while they may be of benefit to their student bodies, they function beyond the realm of an open marketplace. The majority of students enrolled in the programs have simply elected to stay. These schools should not, therefore, be considered as alternatives from the standpoint of program marketing, although they do bolster the system's head-count of students involved in alternative education. (Sometimes, alas, this head-count is an end in itself.)

Since it is possible and often desirable to replicate certain types of

Magnet Schools at multiple sites (many districts have numerous IGE schools, for example), a central location is not as important a consideration for most neighborhood Magnets as it is for neutral-site schools. Multiple neighborhood-Magnet sites are often desirable since Magnets are frequently set up in facilities where the pre-existent student population is of a single race. When only one Magnet exists, the only outside applicants admitted, if racial composition is considered, will be those whose race is the minority race at that Magnet School. Multiple sites can ensure non-racially biased district-wide accessibility.

Recruiting a limited number of predominantly black, at-large students for a neighborhood Magnet located in a predominantly white neighborhood is usually easy—so long as the Magnet is not too geographically remote from minority students. Recruiting white students into a black majority neighborhood Magnet School, however, can present a challenge; and the effort frequently results in only limited success. This is particularly true if only white students from white majority schools are eligible to apply because of the black majority already at the school.

Ideally, in short, a neighborhood Magnet should be set up at a site with substantial excess capacity where the pre-existent student body is already racially balanced to a degree. Converting schools that are already racially balanced into Magnets provides the "controls" necessary to ensure that the school can retain its racial balance, and yet still accept outside applicants of more than one race.

3. *School-Within-A-School Magnet or Alternative*

    a. *Definition:* Schools-within-schools are unique either in structure or in subject emphasis, but in either case they operate in the same building(s) as a neighborhood school. Schools-within-schools are open to district-wide enrollment, and no prior right of admission is given to students already enrolled within the host school. Like neutral-site schools, a school-within-a-school almost always stresses a unique content focus or supplement. It is usually "grown"— that is, it is initiated at any entry level grade and then is permitted to grow vertically each year with the addition of a new grade. Recruiting for a school-within-a-Magnet or alternative, is, therefore, primarily intended to replace the entry level class.

    b. *Site Selection:* Like neighborhood Magnets, schools-within-schools require host schools with ample excess capacity. Similarly, specific types of schools-within-schools can be replicated at multiple sites. Although these programs are usually content-oriented, the form they assume within a host school usually limits their growth potential at a single site, thereby necessitating multiple sites to serve the market adequately.

Since schools-within-schools are self-contained programs within a host school, yet open to district-wide enrollment, they are frequently set up at racially isolated host schools. While the establishment of a school-within-a-school in a racially isolated host school cannot integrate the school *per se,* it does serve to foster a more racially mixed overall educational setting. As grades are added, quite often the school-within-a-school becomes more dominant than the neighborhood school, affording the district the opportunity either to pair attendance areas or to absorb the existing attendance area into contiguous zones. In fact, when neighborhood attendance becomes small enough, one of the above courses of action becomes almost mandatory.

Like neutral-site schools, schools-within-schools are usually initiated at centrally located sites—usually in predominantly minority schools. Once market demand for a particular type of alternative program has been achieved, though, the program can be replicated at one or more sites in outlying sections throughout the district.

B. STUDENT TRANSPORTATION

Providing bus service to alternatives is an absolute essential if all students are to be given an equal opportunity to attend and participate. In most instances, student transportation to and from alternatives requires a separate system of buses and routes which exclusively serve alternative students. The neighborhood school that the student would otherwise attend is usually used as a pick-up point, with service being provided from there to the alternative sites.

Transit time, not distance *per se,* is the essential factor to be considered in a program marketing and student recruitment strategy. If one-way transit time exceeds forty minutes, parent/student eagerness to participate tends to diminish rapidly.

All too frequently, student transportation becomes the Achilles' heel of alternative education. Poorly designed and/or under-used systems can easily result in long transit times and excessive per capita transit costs, both of which can severly hamper a district's willingness and ability to sustain alternative programs. In this regard, it is essential that alternative education be permitted to develop to a point where sufficient numbers of students are involved to allow for cost-effective use of transit systems.

C. FUNCTIONAL RELATIONSHIPS BETWEEN ALTERNATIVES

In certain respects, alternative education should be regarded as a sub-system of a district, rather than as a collection of individual neutral-site schools, neighborhood Magnet Schools, and Magnet programs. Whenever possible, alternative education should be developed to the point where "feeder alternatives" serving elementary students are established which will automatically "feed" other alternative schools made up of secondary students. This does not necessarily mean that elementary alternatives must be continued into the secondary school level. It does, however, suggest that patterns be developed which encourage students enrolled in elementary alternatives to continue with related secondary alternatives. This natural transition is enhanced if the "break points" between alternatives involve grade levels different from those in traditional schools. For example, in a district with K-6 elementary schools, 7-8 Junior Highs, and 9-12 Senior Highs, two functionally related alternatives could serve grades 4-9 as well as 10-12.

From the standpoint of student recruitment, the simplest alternative system to sustain is one that permits recruiting efforts to be concentrated at a single grade level (district-wide). The reason for this is that students, once enrolled in an alternative, are enabled to stay with alternatives throughout their entire school life. Conversely, an alternative system that must virtually re-populate itself every other year, requires an intensive, continuous recruiting effort which is beyond the capacity of most districts.

In Cincinnati, to cite one case, the performing arts school gets a new fourth grade each year, while the bilingual programs get new first grades. Similarly, in St. Louis, the Visual and Performing Arts Center recruits a new fifth grade each year, but, in this case the break between the Center (the lower-grade program) and the Visual and Performing Arts High School corresponds to the city-wide division between grades eight and nine. Consequently, it does not assure the continuity a different break-point might have. It is quite easy for a student to "return" at grade nine to his district school.

As for Dallas, it began its major, and very successful, effort at the high school level. Still, if Dallas does not develop some logical "feeder" programs (*e.g.*, an arts program to prepare students for the arts magnet), it could well find its energies diminishing after a time from the sheer effort required to recruit a sufficient number of new secondary students each year. For at least two reasons, high school students appear to be more reluctant to leave their home schools than are lower grade students: 1) they are less easily influenced by their parents than are smaller children, and 2) they become heavily involved in student activities and so are more subject to peer pressures.

D. STUDENT ELIGIBILITY AND ENTRANCE REQUIREMENTS

Ideally, all students attending regular schools within a district should be eligible to apply for all alternatives serving their grade levels. The imposition of eligibility requirements, in any form, serves only to reduce the number of students able to participate, thereby artificially restricting the growth potential and equality of alternative education.

The two most prevalent forms of eligibility requirements are *racial* and *geographic*. Racial eligibility sometimes dictates that a student is not eligible for an alternative school *if* such acceptance would adversely affect the racial composition of the "sending school" (*i.e.,* the school he's coming from). Indeed, in some instances, students residing within the district and attending non-public schools have been deemed ineligible simply because they were of the same race as the minority group at the neighborhood school which they *would* have attended had they previously been enrolled within that district. This is clearly absurd. Unfortunately, though, alternatives dependent upon federal funding are subject to racial eligibility requirements which emphasize short-term efficacy, and overlook the long-term potential alternatives have for reducing racial isolation.

The other important eligibility requirement is the establishment of geographical attendance areas within the district. With the possible exception of very large districts, an attendance area that comprises less than the entire district serves to limit artificially the market for alternatives; it further suggests that an alternative is only a special type of neighborhood school. The only defensible bases for geographic restrictions are the high per capita cost and the excessive time required to transport a few students over comparatively long distances. These higher costs, however, should temporarily be tolerated whenever possible, in the hope of either replicating the alternative at additional sites or recruiting additional students from remote parts of the district.

Entrance requirements, by definition, contradict the essential voluntary character of alternative education. Indeed, schools or programs with entrance requirements—particularly those employing criteria which can only be applied by the district's professional staff—should not really be considered alternatives. Rather, they should be viewed as special programs, with a student admission policy subject to a relatively formal counseling and evaluation process. Programs which by their very nature can be assumed to serve a certain population—*e.g.,* persons having past experience with Juvenile Courts, drop-outs, or pregnant teenagers—cannot be considered as alternatives because of their unique entrance requirements. In many cases, students there are given no option; the district says, "attend this school 'for your type' or none at all."

The use of teacher recommendations, informal interviews, auditions, and, in certain instances, past achievement records (for accelerated or college preparatory alternatives), do not constitute entrance requirements *per se*. Instead, they are mechanisms that can and should be employed to ascertain whether a student applicant has the aptitude and ability to benefit from a particular alternative. Such mechanisms, therefore, should not be employed in determining student eligibility, but only as tools which professional educators may use in the counseling of parents and students about an appropriate school choice. But, to reiterate, the great majority of alternatives should have *no* requirements for entry, and students should be accepted on a first-come, first-served basis—subject only to age, grade-level, and racial quotas at the *receiving* school.

Student Recruitment

A. INTERPRETATION

As defined earlier, student recruitment constitutes a direct sales effort. Its principal objective is the generation of eligible student applications for an alternative program. Once received, these applications are invariably "processed" to ensure racially balanced alternatives and compliance with program requirements, if any. Not until then is the applicant formally accepted.

It is worth remembering that an eligible application represents no more than a student's intent to participate in a program and is subject to his or her final confirmation. If the district controls acceptance, it is the student applicant who reserves the final right to confirm this acceptance. In short, since both parties can, in effect, stop eligible applications from becoming enrolled students, an application should not necessarily be considered as equivalent to an enrolled student. For this reason, the ultimate success of a student recruitment campaign is measured by the number of eligible applications that finally become enrolled students.

To ensure success, the student recruitment process must of necessity focus upon sincerely interested students who will be accepted, and should avoid over-soliciting students who will probably not be accepted or whose interest is marginal.

B. GENERAL STUDENT RECRUITMENT

The primary objectives of a general student recruitment campaign are to communicate the existence of the district's alternatives, and to provide a means whereby interested students can apply. The principal communication vehicle used for general student recruitment is the alternative brochure. A typical brochure contains details about the site, descriptions of each alternative offered, the grades served, and the program requirements, if any. It also provides answers to such key questions as: "Who is eligible to apply?", "How may applications be processed?", and "How will students be transported?" The major component of the brochure is the application form, which should be detachable and returnable (in person or by mail) to the district's administrative offices. Finally, to ensure fair treatment of all eligible students, the brochures should be distributed district-wide and at one time, preferably by mail to students' homes.

Electronic and print media should also be used as part of the recruitment campaign, but not in lieu of a separately distributed brochure. Since city-wide media probably have already covered the planning of alternatives prior to the initiation of the recruiting process, media coverage at the time the brochures are distributed should be concurrent so as to impress upon students and their parents the need to apply quickly.

Radio and TV stations can be encouraged to carry public service announcements (PSA's) promoting interest in alternatives. In many instances, local newspapers are willing to reprint the brochure (in insert or full-page form) at nominal cost. Both of these recruitment methods give students residing within (or, in some cases, outside) the district, who do not attend public schools, the opportunity to apply.

Broad-based interpretation of the district's alternative program to the public at large, as well as to a variety of interested parties, is another major component of any general recruitment effort. These generally take the form of presentations by the superintendent or other ranking administrators to PTA's, the business community, and important community organizations.

C. FOCUSED STUDENT RECRUITMENT

Many districts, unfortunately, act as if *general* student recruitment and *focused* student recruitment are synonymous. They are not. A general recruitment campaign, of and by itself, is not usually sufficient to prompt the majority of potential candidates to apply to the program. Instead, it tends to generate applications from only the most interested and/or frustrated students (*i.e.,* those who wish to get out of the schools they're attending). However, if student participation in alternatives is to be broad-based and truly representative of the district's entire eligible population, a *focused* recruitment effort is required.

Focused student recruitment is principally concerned with achieving matchups between potentially interested students and specific alternatives. Within the context of the total recruitment campaign, it tends to come after the general recruitment effort. Indeed, the entire recruitment process can be conceived of as an "election" which allows for votes (applications) to be cast over an extended period of time. The first votes to be cast and counted are those applications that result from the *general* student recruitment effort. These early returns are usually complete within two weeks after the original distribution of the alternative brochure. Once these applications have been processed, those responsible for enrolling students should determine the *focused* recruitment effort that will be necessary to generate additionally needed applications. During the remainder of the overall recruitment campaign, each alternative can be filled to capacity (or as near to that as possible) by some form of focused student recruitment.

In short, then, focused student recruitment is concerned with developing a market for *specific* alternatives, while general student recruitment is concerned with *all* alternatives. This distinction is critical, and the judgment as to when and how to shift from promoting the whole program to the promotion of a specific area can affect the ultimate success or failure of the entire recruitment campaign.

One of the best tools available for focused recruitment is teacher and principal recommendations. Prior to the implementation of new alternatives, the nature of the programs should be fully explained to the district's instructional personnel and principals, and they in turn should be requested to submit the names of the students whom they believe would most benefit from specific alternatives. These students and/or their parents can then be contacted as part of the focused recruitment effort.

Still other approaches which can be considered within the context of a focused recruitment campaign are: newspaper, radio, and TV advertisements for *particular* alternatives; news conferences, featuring officials from organizations that plan to become involved with specific content-oriented alternatives; a phone bank staffed by parent volunteers who call eligible students to inform them about two or three specific alternatives; and well-publicized community or district-wide meetings that afford potentially interested students and parents the opportunity to learn more about specific alternatives.

Finally, a meeting of potential students and their parents with program staff can be particularly effective. Since, in many instances, the alternative may not yet be in operation, a prospective student's decision to apply might be determined by his or her confidence in the program's staff. For this reason, alternative principals, program coordinators, and alternative teachers, who are ultimately responsible for delivering the program, are the best possible persons to have at such a meeting.

CONCLUSION

At least four reasons exist for the establishment of alternatives:

1. To improve the quality of instruction
2. To give parents and students a choice, since no one program can satisfy the needs and aspirations of all students
3. To reduce racial isolation through voluntary means
4. To retain (in our cities) or to attract (to our cities) a middle-income, tax-paying constituency.

Before any of these four goals can be realized, however, a required number of students must sign up for alternatives. School systems, therefore, must be very concerned with marketing their programs. The success of such programs is too important to the future of our cities for administrators to hide behind rationalizations like, "We can help create the programs, but it is the responsibility of parents to make the final decision without any influence from us." For the most part, parents do not really understand the opportunities offered them unless they are approached directly by an educational "salesperson."

Administrators must also take risks. If a program is really "better" *for certain students,* administrators should label it as such and clearly explain the reasons for that label. No program will be better for all students.

So as not to be drained by a full-scale recruitment campaign each year, school boards and administrators must make intelligent decisions about alternatives (what will sell and where it will be best merchandized). Similarly, they must be willing to begin the alternative movement in elementary schools and allow it to grow from there. The genius of the Cincinnati system is that almost all the alternatives extend to grade twelve, even though some programs start at kindergarten, and others at grade one, grade four, grade seven, and grade nine. In other words, once a youngster is enrolled in an integrated alternative program, it is important to keep him. This eliminates, among other things, the need to recruit him again. Furthermore, it is easier to interest parents and their children at the elementary level.

During a campaign, general recruitment is followed by a focused effort. In St. Louis, for example, the general effort resulted in hundreds more black applicants than could effectively be served. A focused effort, therefore, was then directed totally at the white population. Without this latter effort, very few (if any) programs would have opened in St. Louis.

A final word. Alternatives should be for everyone. Why tell a future Caruso that he cannot attend a performing arts school because of the racial composition of his *home* school? The racial composition of the alternative or Magnet School should be a major concern of the system. If it is fifty-fifty black-white (as it was in both Cincinnati and St. Louis), the child will be receiving a bi-racial educational experience in the school of his choice. How can *that* be improved upon?

Once, when we were nearing capacity in a Cincinnati alternative, and the racial composition could not tolerate even one more black applicant, we told a black child to go find a white child and return. You know what? He did.

Legal Implications of Magnet Schools

7

Legal Implications of Magnet Schools

GEORGE EDWARDS

Introduction

In the chapter that follows, Judge George Edwards presents a ringing history of segregation and its effects on the citizens of our nation. Speaking primarily of the need – not the methods used – to integrate schools, Judge Edwards says: "No court . . . to my knowledge has rejected alternative schools designed to fit particular needs of particular students without regard to race."

There were two strong motivations for my agreeing to make this speech. First, it gave me one more chance (however brief) to come back home to Dallas — to come back, in the parlance of this period, to my "roots." Second, it gives me a chance to share some of my thoughts about public education with an important group of educational leaders who may be able to do something about this nation's public school problems.

My family has deep roots in Dallas. Indeed, we are meeting within hailing distance of the family pasture which my grandfather bought in 1876 and where my father had the daily task all through his boyhood of taking the family cows to pasture. If that sounds pastoral, Dad's long years in Dallas did not continue that way. He came back from Sewanee and Harvard with a missionary zeal to make things better for the poor and the oppressed, including Blacks. For over fifty years he practiced a unique brand of law on Main Street in Dallas. It was what we might now call poverty law, labor law, and ACLU and NAACP-type law. Those labels had not even been invented then. Not surprisingly, his practice mustered little approbation from the establishment of Dallas.

In 1910, Dad was assigned by the court to defend a Negro charged with a capital offense. His first criminal case ended abruptly when a lynch mob broke through police lines in the old Dallas County Court House, seized the elderly Negro man, put a rope around his neck, and threw the end of the rope to the mob surrounding the Court House, which pulled him out of the second-story window and dragged him up Main Street to Akard. There, to the cheers of the surrounding mob, his body was hung to an arch, built to mark the Elks Convention. So far as I know, my father was the only person in the Dallas of that day who printed an outright (and vehement!) condemnation of the lynching.

That, of course, was before I was born. But my father's life did not grow less adventurous. When I was fifteen, he was kidnapped by the Ku Klux Klan from the steps of the Dallas City Hall where he had gone to get two young clients out of jail after they had been convicted for vagrancy because they were preaching about organizing Black and white labor into one union. The two young men were tarred and feathered, tied to trees in the Trinity River bottoms, and then beaten unconscious. Dad was released unharmed late at night on a country road. He had been warned repeatedly not to talk about the matter. That was a little like telling the Trinity River not to flood in the spring.

Some years ago I wrote, and W.W. Norton published, a book entitled *Pioneer at Law*. It was about my father and my roots in Dallas. Its sale hardly rivaled Alex Haley's *Roots* but, like Haley, I found that reliving my progenitors' lives was a fascinating experience.

One more reminiscence: Both my mother and my father taught in the Dallas Public Schools in the years immediately after they graduated from college. So I grew up in a home which (after love of God and fellow-man) held education and books in the highest esteem. Dad and Mother founded, and then taught as volunteers in, the Dallas public night school. The fee which will be paid me for making this speech will go to the recently created Dallas Public Library's Memorial Fund for my father, and to Christ Church Episcopal in Cincinnati for summer camp scholarships for the Appalachian and Black children of Peaslee School where, for the past ten years, my wife has taught remedial reading as a volunteer teacher's aide. Incidentally, in 1976, 69 percent of Peaslee's students, who come from the poorest neighborhood in downtown Cincinnati, ranked average or above average in reading. Peg and I feel privileged to be associated with the dedicated group of teachers at Peaslee who accomplish this kind of result in a neighborhood which most of middle-class America would think unpromising, to say the least. We also feel privileged to be associated with Don Waldrip, who, as Superintendent of Cincinnati Schools, afforded leadership to Cincinnati's reading improvement program, as well as to its alternative schools program, which I know has been the direct focus of this conference.

I came here today to say three things, really. First, we must, if our cherished way of life is to be preserved, find the means to bring this nation together as one America. Not Black America. Not Hispanic America. Not White America. *One America!*

Second, we must find a different and better way to finance our impossibly burdened and impoverished public schools.

Third, to accomplish both these objectives, we need to open our minds to new thoughts and to new solutions — alternative solutions, if you will.

As a judge, I have limitations which I try never to forget. For example, I cannot discuss cases pending or likely to be pending in my court. And I assure you, I shall not. But no judge loses his rights or duties as a citizen when he takes the bench. And, from our dockets, we see so much in such depth and in such detail. Many times I feel like the pathologist in the laboratory of a hospital basement looking at a frozen-section slide of an unconscious patient somewhere upstairs. As judges, we read in our records the frozen-section slides on the body politic of America. Let me briefly describe, then, the dangerous growth that I see — and something of its origin.

The greatest domestic problem of today began long before this country became a nation. In 1619, a Dutch ship landed at Jamestown in the British colony of Virginia. It carried twenty Negro slaves from the coast of Africa. By the outbreak of the Civil War, 241 years later, it is estimated that there were four million slaves in the United States. All of these, as well as their progenitors, had been brought here in the holds of slave ships sailing the infamous Middle Passage from Africa to the Americas. That Passage, where millions of captive Africans suffered and hundreds of thousands died in torture, is one of history's worst examples of man's inhumanity to man.

On a typical slave ship, the between decks hold where slaves were kept was anywhere from three and one-half to five feet high. The slaves were therefore compelled to lie "spoon fashion." The space was divided on the basis of eighteen inches by five and one-half feet. Every man (though not the women and children) was ironed to another man and then to a bar running the length of the hold. There were no sanitary facilities. The presence of a slave ship on the open ocean was frequently made known by its stench, long before its topsails could be seen. If provisions ran low on a bad voyage, the sick or the weak among the slaves were thrown overboard so as to divide the remaining food among those most likely to survive. Depending on wind and weather, the voyage from the African slave coast to the East coast of America might take anywhere from one month to three months. It is estimated that 20 percent of all the slaves who embarked died during the sea voyage.

One could wish that a much better report could be made on slavery in the early colonies and then later, after independence. There are, of course, many individual instances of kind masters and cherished slaves. Such stories, however, pertain almost exclusively to house servants and not to field hands who comprised the great majority of the slaves. The fact is that slavery as an institution treated human beings as wholly-owned physical property — disposable at the will, whim, and caprice of the master. Until the Emancipation Proclamation of 1863, slaves had no legal rights in courts. It was a crime to perform a marriage ceremony between two slaves. The master had a right to breed the female slave to the male slave *he* chose for her. He also had a right to use the female slaves for his own sexual gratification — and, if we compare African skin color to the skin color of American "Blacks," we know how often that privilege was exercised. Fathers among the slaves had no rights at all in relation to their children, if they even had a relationship. Slave mothers usually reared their young — but their children could be, and frequently were, sold away from them like any other animal produce. Guns, chains, whips, and bloodhounds were the means of enforcing slavery. Up to the very end of the Civil War, black-skinned men, women, and children were treated by law like animals rather than human beings.

It would, of course, distort history if one failed to note here that there were those who protested. Though the growth of abolition was slow and faltering, in time the numbers supporting it grew to be legion.

The most inspiring and prophetic sentence in American history was written in 1776. It still haunts us 200 years later. In the Declaration of Independence, Jefferson wrote:

> *We hold these truths to be self-evident, that all men are created equal, that they are endowed by their Creator with certain unalienable Rights, that among these are Life, Liberty and the pursuit of Happiness.*

Viewed in the context of its times, this was a strange assertion. Nothing really could have been less self-evident under the rule of George III of England. This was a declaration of revolt against absolute monarchy, made with high hope at the time of the founding of the first nation dedicated to equality of man in the history of the world.

Implicit, though ignored in that ringing phrase and in the Constitution which followed, was the deadly contradiction to which we have already referred. The equality Americans sought was not extended to their Negro slaves. The Constitution itself made this clear. It contained matter-of-fact references to the institution of slavery, even though it did not employ the actual word. Where the context made clear that the reference was to slaves, it employed the term ''persons'' — a term likewise employed to describe all citizens of the new country.

Those who drafted these documents clearly knew what they were doing. Three Virginians — Jefferson, Madison, and Mason — were among the most influential drafters of the Declaration of Independence, the Constitution, and the Bill of Rights. All three were thinkers and philosophers far ahead of their time. All in the face of hopeless odds repeatedly expressed their opposition both to the slave trade and slavery. Though they owned slaves themselves, it seems likely that they wrote with deliberation and that they meant in God's own time for the unqualified declarations of equality and freedom to apply to Black as well as to white, to slave as well as to free man. It is equally clear that the large majority of the Constitutional Convention did not share that intention.

During the first ninety years of the Republic, the courts, when dealing with cases involving slavery, found the ''freedom'' language of the Bill of Rights to be indigestible material. The answer lay in redefining terms. The use of the word ''person'' in the Constitution was ignored. Slaves, for purposes of the law, were not citizens; they were not even men. They were chattels; they were things. In fact, for Chief Justice Taney of the Civil War Supreme Court, even a *freed* slave remained in a sub-human class — a thing less than a citizen — less than a man. Most historians believe that the Dred Scott decision which Taney wrote made the Civil War inevitable.

Let us pause to take note of the tragedy of that conflict. When North fought South — at least in part over slavery — more men died in that conflict than have died in all the other wars in which the United States has engaged. The Civil War cost 617,000 dead — 359,000 from the North, 258,000 from the South.

At the end of that war, the Emancipation Proclamation — followed by the Thirteenth, Fourteenth, and Fifteenth Amendments — made clear that the release of the Negro from slavery and his restoration to full citizenship was one of the fundamental war aims and results.

Those in Congress who wrote the Thirteenth and Fourteenth Amendments sought to make this fact clear. The Thirteenth Amendment abolished slavery. The Fourteenth Amendment made all persons born in the United States citizens. It then provided that "No State shall make or enforce any law which shall abridge the privileges or immunities of citizens of the United States; nor shall any State deprive any person of life, liberty, or property, without due process of law; nor deny to any person within its jurisdiction the equal protection of the laws."

When we re-read these words, we are led to wonder how — if we were now to undertake the task — we could devise words more specifically designed to establish and command complete equality for all persons under the law of our land.

For a brief time, in the immediate aftermath of the Civil War and the Reconstruction Period, the Fourteenth Amendment was actually read clearly and enforced. For example, a West Virginia law prohibiting Black jurors was struck down, as was a Louisville, Kentucky, ordinance banning Negro citizens from residing in certain sections of the city.

A long hiatus followed, however. Congress found the Reconstruction Period a long, bitter, and expensive experience. The abolitionists of the North, having won their legal victory, lost followers and enthusiasm. And, in the South, bitter men who had met but never accepted defeat organized the Ku Klux Klan and lynch law, as a way of repealing in actual fact the hated amendments which they could not legally strike from the books. Between the Civil War and the 1940's, there were probably 5,000 lynchings.

Segregation, the Klan's substitute for slavery, had never been a part of the pre-Civil War Southern culture. The freest of contact and association had been the rule between master and servant. Slavery served not only to define the station of each, but also to make clear the inferior status of the slave. Once slavery was legally dead, however, segregation was needed in order to reassert Negro inferiority and to require him to accept inferior facilities in every aspect of his life.

By 1896, segregation as a system had prevailed overwhelmingly and had been written into the laws of all of the Southern states. In practice, though, segregation had penetrated the entire nation.

In that same year, the United States Supreme Court found itself confronted with the first constitutional test of segregation by a state. In *Plessy v. Ferguson* [163 U.S. 537 (1896)], a man named Plessy, seven-eighths white by birth, went into a railroad compartment reserved by Louisiana law to whites. He was arrested and charged with being a Negro and, hence, in violation of the Louisiana railroad segregation law. It was established to the satisfaction of the Louisiana courts that one of Plessy's eight great-grandparents had been Negro, and he was convicted. Plessy's appeal seems to have been directed primarily at the illogic of the

Louisiana view that the "inferior" Negro was so potent that just one Negro great-grandparent could outweigh seven white great-grandparents.

In the end, the United States Supreme Court found this Louisiana view of the facts to be permissible. It then turned its attention to the Fourteenth Amendment, which Plessy had raised almost as if by afterthought.

The mandatory language of the amendment gave the Court little trouble. It simply assumed the inferiority of the Negro as a fact, and proceeded from there to reason that, when the law recognized this fact, no damage was done.

Just as there were brave men who fought (and sometimes died fighting) against the Ku Klux Klan and lynch law, so there were such men in the courts. John Marshall Harlan's dissent in *Plessy* made sure that all who read would know that both the Fourteenth Amendment and its doctrine of equality and freedom had been betrayed by the Supreme Court, which was their legal guardian.

The majority opinion — which all the justices except Harlan signed — held that, where facilities for the races were equal, the law could require them to be separate. And it went on to illustrate its point by reference to separate schools for Negro and white children.

What followed in the aftermath of this decision represents tortured pages of legal history. The *Plessy* "separate-but-equal" rule produced some ludicrous, if not obscene, results in a subsequent series of cases. These included the criminal indictment and conviction of Berea College, because its founders' understanding of Christianity required them to teach Negro as well as white students without discrimination. In another case, confronted by the fact that Oklahoma had no Negro graduate schools even under the *Plessy* doctrine, the Court was forced to rule that a qualified Negro student had to be accepted. Oklahoma complied by seating one Black graduate student named McLaurin in an anteroom off the classroom marked "Reserved for Negroes."

While these cases were haunting the conscience of the Court, the fact was that, in most Southern states and cities, not even the vaguest pretense was made to comply with the *Plessy* doctrine. Separate schools there were for white and Negro children. But equal, they were not.

In 1954, after protracted argument, the Supreme Court finally overruled *Plessy* in *Brown v. the School Board of Topeka*. Interestingly, it did so in a relatively brief opinion. Written by Chief Justice Earl Warren, the opinion was notable for its clarity and for the fact that it was signed by *all* of the Justices of the Court, including three from Southern states.

The Warren opinion attacked the "separate-but-equal" doctrine directly, citing authority for the proposition that there could be no such thing.

> We conclude that in the field of public education the doctrine of "separate but equal" has no place. Separate educational facilities are inherently unequal. Therefore, we hold that the plaintiffs and others similarly situated for whom the actions have been brought are, by reason of the segregation complained of, deprived of the equal protection of the laws guaranteed by the Fourteenth Amendment.

The Court ordered the dismantling of the dual school systems of the South, as well as the desegregation of schools which were segregated on the basis of race. Some of the cases which followed and grew out of this decision include:

Cooper v. Aaron – where President Eisenhower ultimately sent federal troops to Little Rock, Arkansas, to confront a defiant governor.

Green v. County School Board – where the Supreme Court demanded a school board desegregation plan which "promises realistically to work now."

Swann v. Charlotte-Mecklenburg Board of Education – where Chief Justice Burger wrote the following for a unanimous Court:

> The decree provided that the buses used to implement the Plan would operate on direct routes. Students would be picked up at schools near their homes and transported to the schools they were to attend. The trips for elementary school pupils average about seven miles and the District Court found that they would take "not over 35 minutes at the most." This system compares favorably with the transportation plan previously operated in Charlotte under which each day 23,600 students on all grade levels were transported an average of 15 miles one way for an average trip requiring over an hour. In these circumstances, we find no basis for holding that the local school authorities may not be required to employ bus transportation as one tool of school desegregation. Desegregation plans cannot be limited to the walk-in school.

Keyes v. School District No. 1 Denver – where the Supreme Court found segregation supported by state and local action and so applied its desegregation order to the entire school system.

Bradley v. Milliken – where the Supreme Court affirmed that a segregated school system in Detroit was unconstitutional but, by a 5-4 vote, rejected planning for metropolitan area desegregation because, in its view, the proofs of state and suburban discrimination were not sufficient to justify such a remedy.

And, finally, the more recent cases in Louisville, Kentucky; Wilmington, Delaware; and Indianapolis, Indiana — where on proofs of area discrimination which the Supreme Court considered stronger, areawide desegregation plans were approved. But see *Austin Independent School District v. United States* [45 USLW 3413 (U.S. Dec. 7, 1976)].

I know that many people today talk as if America's race problem could be summed up in just one word, "busing." Let us be clear, though, about how we use language and history. Busing of school students started long before the Supreme Court told the country that segregated schools were unconstitutional. Until the late 1960's, the overwhelming majority (in fact, almost all) of the students being bused were white students to white schools — and everybody thought that was fine. It was *only* when the courts began to use busing as "one of the tools" of desegregation, in the words of Chief Justice Burger, that protest arose. Let's be frank about it. It is not the school bus that is the problem. It's who is on the bus — and where the bus is going — that counts. When Black children were provided with bus transportation to previously all-white schools, or vice versa, "busing" suddenly became anathema. The Ku Klux Klan burned buses in Pontiac, Michigan, on the day school opened there under a desegregation order, and a number of its members were convicted for this. But, the KKK doesn't hate buses. What it has always merchandised is the hatred of Blacks.

I suggest that the very fate of America, and even the fate of democracy in the world, may depend upon this nation's ability to quell the fires of race hatred which organizations like the Ku Klux Klan and its cohorts have engendered.

How can I best tell you of my concern for your success in your deliberations today? I am, like all judges, sworn to follow and uphold the Constitution of the United States. But I also am one who believes in it. I consider it the shining example of man's best hope in a difficult world. With George Mason of Virginia, I feel that, when our forefathers wrote the Constitution and the Bill of Rights, they were walking on "enchanted ground." But even if I had doubts about the wisdom of our forefathers, I would still feel that their inspiring words made exceedingly practical sense for the America of today.

Let me tell you what I see around me. I see an increasingly segregated America. I see a strange and dangerous kind of apartheid developing, a pattern which is being replicated in most of our biggest cities. The white population's move to the suburbs increasingly leaves the inner cities to the Blacks. If current trends continue, we may have — in a decade or so — a dozen or more cities with ninety percent or more of their residents Black.

We could not, even if we wanted to, create a more dangerous situation than this — namely, the downtown district owned by whites and occupied by them by the thousands upon thousands in daytime hours; the rest of the central city occupied by Black residents; the central city surrounded by a white suburban ring in a state equally dominated by whites. And if you add to this picture a large white majority of policemen, firemen, and school teachers dealing with crime and fires and school children in heavily Black neighborhoods where the youth has the highest percentage of unemployment in America, you have all the ingredients necessary for race conflict. Indeed, it may finally come to a domestic conflict comparable almost to a second Civil War.

I am not one who accepts the inevitability of evil. Mankind and, yes, especially this nation of ours, has the capacity, I believe, for intelligent and compassionate action — the sort of action which has brought you all here today. I could not refuse your invitation to speak to this meeting, simply because I am so grateful that some group has the good sense to consider the problems facing us and to plan for possible solutions.

And there, my friends, is where the judicial branch of government is almost powerless. In this country, as in no other country in the world, our courts are guardians of the conscience of the country as it was expressed in the Constitution. Yet they are called upon to pass judgment on what has happened, rather than to make plans for improvement or to avoid disaster.

The most dangerous thing in America today is that concern about the problem of race has been focused almost solely in our judicial branch of government, while the executive and legislative branches have been studiously looking the other way. We can only hope that this will change.

Problems of race are not the only pressures in public schools today. Of utmost importance to the public schools is a new look at school financing. The real estate tax, for example, no longer provides an adequate basis for public school support. Local tax levy elections, which control much school financing, involve so many diverse motivations on the part of voters as to generally produce disastrous results. I suggest that public education is as vital to the future of this country as is national defense. In this increasingly complex world, the future of our young depends upon education. For that very reason, so does the future of our country. Yet, when we ask hard-pressed teachers in inner city schools to teach thirty to thirty-five students in a classroom, we demean the concept of learning. Over-reliance upon local property taxes may mean that the sort of inequality of education which the Supreme Court found in dual school systems will come back to haunt us — only this time in the form of too disparate a contrast between suburban and central city schools.

Both federal and state governments should act now to provide funds for quality education, particularly in the cities where the declining tax base is heading us toward indefensibly unequal school systems. Similarly, both federal and state governments should recognize the need for smaller classroom sizes (less than twenty students per teacher) — particularly in the early grades, and particularly in the most economically depressed areas.

New means to alleviate, or cure our educational problems must constantly be sought. Your conference on Magnet or alternative schools is one such effort. I am, of course, well aware that sometimes a voluntary transfer scheme in school systems has been proposed simply as a way to avoid realistic desegregation. The Supreme Court has constantly reminded us that a true desegregation plan is one which promises to work and to "work now."

To my knowledge, however, no court has rejected alternative schools designed to meet particular needs of particular students without regard to race. Certainly, alternative schools that are slanted toward the performing arts, or to specialization in mathematics, science, or language can draw students, regardless of race, creed, color or geographical location. In fact, alternatives may prove to be one of the innovative ideas which lead in the direction of better education for *all* of our young people. For is it not also possible for such schools to serve not only the inner city but the suburbs as well?

I cannot conclude without some reference to jobs and housing, even if it has to be of the briefest sort.

Both federal and state governments should recognize the desperate need for a Jobs for Youth program in cities where unemployment among Black youth has reached staggering proportions. What was done in the 1930's, in the worst of America's depressions, can surely be done again. And I note that President Carter has recently made a beginning in this direction.

In the *Hills v. Gautreaux* case (1976) the Supreme Court pointed toward the feasibility of desegregation of housing in segregated suburban areas. Those who know the history of housing over the past forty years know about the role the Federal Housing Agency played in developing the segregated suburbs and, in turn, our present problem of increasing apartheid. The executive and legislative branches could employ the same agency to undo the damage it has done.

Ten years ago, the Supreme Court pointed out in *Jones v. Mayer Company* that "At the very least, the freedom that Congress is empowered to secure under the Thirteenth Amendment includes the freedom to buy whatever a white man can buy, the right to live wherever a white man can live. If Congress cannot say that being a free man means at least this much, then the Thirteenth Amendment made a promise the Nation cannot keep."

In closing, I turn to an authority from still more ancient history — Romans 13:8-12:

> Owe no man any thing, but to love one another: for he that loveth another hath fulfilled the law.
>
> For this, thou shalt not commit adultery, thou shalt not kill, thou shalt not steal, thou shalt not bear false witness, thou shalt not covet; and if there be any other commandment, it is briefly comprehended in this saying, namely, thou shalt love thy neighbour as thyself.
>
> Love worketh no ill to his neighbour: therefore love is the fulfilling of the Law.
>
> And that, knowing the time, that now it is high time to awake out of sleep: for now is our salvation nearer than when we first believed.
>
> The night is far spent, the day is at hand: let us therefore cast off the works of darkness, and let us put on the armour of light.

Educational Options: What's Happening Today?

8

Educational Options: What's Happening Today?

VERNON H. SMITH

Introduction

Dr. Vernon H. Smith presents here a useful system of categories for public school options, as well as data on the extent of optional school development throughout the nation. In addition, he reports on attendance, achievement, and behavior in optional schools and describes how optional schools are being used as a desegregation strategy. Finally, the author provides a rationale for the development of options.

Approximately 10,000 optional public schools are now in operation, providing choice in public education for families and teachers in about 5,000 American communities. In many other communities, school systems are providing optional programs within the standard schools. And many public schools, both alternative and conventional, are providing optional action-learning experiences outside the school, but for school credit.

Alternative public schools (*i.e.*, "public schools of choice") have grown since 1970 from a few widely scattered, isolated efforts to a point where today most large school systems and even many smaller ones are providing optional schools. This recent burgeoning of optional public schools and programs may in fact be the most significant development in the history of American education.

After more than a decade of efforts to reform the public schools, there appears to be a general realization now that one school cannot meet the needs of all the children or young people within it boundaries. There is an emerging consensus from within the educational profession and from the general public as well that the development of optional public schools may be one way to fulfill our long-term commitment to equality of educational opportunity.

A 1975 survey by the National School Boards Association found that twenty-eight percent of the districts responding had alternative schools in operation. *Over two-thirds of the districts with more than 25,000 students had alternative schools*, as did forty percent of the medium-sized districts and eighteen percent of the small districts. The 1976 NSBA *Research Report: Alternative Schools* concluded that "the alternative school concept is definitely not on the fringe of

American public school activity; it is an important part of the program in many school districts and its significance is growing."

National Recommendations

The concept of the optional public school has gained widespread national support. Since the 1970 White House Conference on Children recommended "immediate, massive funding for the development of alternative optional forms of public education," more than a dozen other national reports on education have endorsed alternative public schools. A 1976 Rand Corporation report, *Youth Policy in Transition*, after analyzing three of these reports, concluded that "underlying all of these proposals is the belief that no one institution, especially the current high school, can meet the needs of an increasingly heterogeneous clientele."

The National Commission on the Reform of Secondary Education urged that "each district should provide a broad range of alternative schools and programs so that every student will have meaningful options available."

The National Association of Secondary School Principals, the National School Boards Association, the North Central Association of Schools and Colleges, Phi Delta Kappa, and the U.S. Office of Education have likewise endorsed the development of optional public schools and programs.

Owen Kiernan, Executive Secretary of the NASSP, pointed out that "in a society as diverse and complex as ours, no institution can effectively serve all people...The fact that we continue to have almost one million high school dropouts each year gives credence to the fact that the standard offerings simply do not meet the needs of all students."

Harold V. Webb, Executive Director of the NSBA, has said "the National School Boards Association encourages boards to seriously consider the concept of alternative public education programs...Options within public school systems exemplify lay control at its best."

The North Central Association's *Policies and Standards for the Approval of Optional Schools and Special Function Schools* stated that "widespread educational options — the coexistence of many types of alternative schools and programs — should strengthen American education as a whole."

A 1976 Phi Delta Kappa Task Force Report, *The New Secondary Education*, recommended alternatives in schooling as a way of providing "suitable choices within the regular system."

The first major recommendation of the USOE's National Panel on High Schools and Adolescent Education was that "the unattained practice and inadequate concept of the comprehensive high school be replaced with the more practical goal of providing comprehensive education through a variety of means including the schools."

Finally, the 1973 Gallup Poll of Public Attitudes Toward Education indicated that over sixty percent of the respondents (including over sixty percent of the parents and over eighty percent of the professional educators) favored the establishment of alternative public schools for "students who are not interested in, or are bored with, the usual kind of education."

Types of Optional Public Schools

Optional alternative public schools vary widely in terms of instruction, curricula, resources, structure, and size (*e.g.*, they range from multi-million-dollar educational parks, such as the Skyline Center in Dallas, to one-room storefront dropout centers). Because there are more than a dozen types of such schools in operation, it is difficult to classify them; however, the following list does provide a general overview of their range:

- *Alternative schools where the focus is on different modes of instruction*: open schools, continuous progress schools, behavior modification schools, Montessori schools, free schools.
- *Alternative schools where the focus is on different curricular modes:* Magnet Schools (a generic term), environmental schools, performing arts schools, multicultural schools, bilingual schools.
- *Alternative schools where the focus is on resources (usually resources that a school district could not provide in every school)*: learning centers, schools-without-walls, vocational high schools, career centers, educational parks.
- *Alternative schools where the focus is on the needs of various clienteles*: continuation schools (a generic term), dropout centers, street academies, evening schools, pregnancy-maternity centers.

Any of the above schools can be found operating in a variety of organizational structures — *e.g.*, as separate autonomous schools, schools-within-schools, mini-schools, satellite schools, or as a network of alternative schools scattered throughout the community.

No Common Cause

The concept of the alternative public school is not new. Throughout our history, communities have provided alternative schools for scattered target groups of students — *i.e.*, evening high schools for employed young adults, special high schools for talented students, vocational and trade high schools for "non-academic" students, and occasional programs for pregnant girls (although many school districts, even today, make no provisions for the quarter of a million school-age girls who become pregnant each year).

is new is the notion that there should be choice in public education for
ly at every grade level. This concept grew, as a 1974 Ford Foundation
report states, "...from the ashes of past attempts at school reform. In the 1960's
the federal government, private foundations, corporations, and community groups
poured massive amounts of money and energy into efforts to change the public
school system.... These large-scale efforts failed to produce large-scale changes,
partly because it is so difficult to make a dent in the public school system."

Other than this common base of educational choice for the student populations they serve, the various optional schools, optional programs, and optional
learning experiences have no common cause and share no common history. Many
of them were grass-roots responses to perceived learning needs within their
communities; still others were the result of some form of outside intervention:
federal and/or state funding, foundation grants, etc. In a few communities, the
development of optional schools was a result of the social upheaval of the late
sixties, just as in a few communities today, the optional fundamental schools are a
result of the back-to-basics conservatism of the mid-seventies.

Current Developments

MAGNET SCHOOLS AND RACIAL INTEGRATION

The optional Magnet Schools in many of our cities, including Dallas, are one
of the results of the integration efforts that followed the Supreme Court's 1954
decision in *Brown v. Topeka*. For several years, optional public schools in
Cleveland, Louisville, and St. Paul have been serving as models for voluntary
integration. In Houston and Pasadena, court-approved school integration plans
include optional public schools.

In 1975, federal judges in Boston and Detroit mandated optional public
schools in their desegregation decisions. Judge W. Arthur Garrity in Boston called
the twenty-two Magnet Schools "the crux and magic" of his school desegregation
plan. In Detroit, U.S. District Court Judge Robert DeMascio ruled that open
enrollment schools and vocational centers would be made available to all Detroit
students, but with controlled racial composition.

The busing controversy has attracted much attention, particularly in Boston
and Louisville. The Brown School in downtown Louisville, an optional open
school, opened its doors even before court-ordered desegregation with a voluntary
half-black, half-white student population. In spite of bitter opposition to *forced*
busing, Brown School continues to operate peacefully, with long waiting lists of
families of both races who want their children to enroll.

Four Constitutional amendments that would end forced busing have recently
been proposed. One of them, the National Equal Opportunities Acts of 1974,
would provide that educational parks and Magnet Schools be established for the
voluntary transfer of students from schools where their race was in a majority to
schools where their race would be in a minority.

FUNDAMENTAL SCHOOLS AND THE BACK-TO-BASICS MOVEMENT

In several communities, public school systems are now providing optional fundamental (back-to-basics) schools to satisfy the concerns of those families who prefer a more conservative school than the standard school.

Fundamental schools usually operate with emphasis on the three R's and patriotism and usually have a parent-approved discipline code. To date, admittedly, the demand for such schools has been slight, but publicity on declining student test scores is creating an increased interest in them. In the 1975 Annual Gallup Poll of Public Attitudes Toward Education, for example, fifty-six percent of parents with school-age children responded that they would enroll their children in an optional alternative public school that emphasized basic skills and discipline.

ALTERNATIVE SCHOOLS AND DECLINING TEST SCORES

The potential of the optional public schools to develop basic skills is greater than that of the few scattered fundamental schools currently in existence. Evaluation reports from a variety of alternative schools consistently indicate that students make more progress in the basic skills in alternative programs than they did in the standard schools. Similarly, a 1974 Ford Foundation report shows that "where standard measures of achievement such as test scores and college admissions are applicable, they show that alternative school students perform at least as well as their counterparts in traditional school programs, and usually better." (This report was not referring to fundamental schools but to other types of alternatives.)

VANDALISM AND VIOLENCE; ABSENTEEISM AND TRUANCY

At present, more money is spent on vandalism and other crimes in the schools than on textbooks and instructional materials. As pointed out, the renewed interest in the fundamental schools is certainly related to parental concern about discipline in the schools. Furthermore, in the annual Gallup Polls of Public Attitudes Toward Education, discipline has been most frequently cited as the major problem confronting the public schools, while among secondary school principals, absenteeism and discipline are rated as the number one and number two problems.

Only a few alternative schools have originated to date as a response to absenteeism or crime. One large urban high school, with a seventy percent truancy rate and a sixty percent dropout rate, was converted to a complex of optional mini-schools in a desperate effort to save the school.

In some communities, disruptive students are being assigned to so-called "alternative schools." Though the segregation and isolation of disruptive students may be desirable or even necessary in these communities, the "alternative school" label is a misnomer. While the school may be an alternative for the assigner, it is certainly not an alternative for the students assigned to it.

Recent state recommendations for the development of smaller optional public schools in California, New York, and Pennsylvania have been based in part on the need to combat increasing crime and absenteeism in the schools. The Task Force on the Resolution of Conflict in California Schools reported that "the incidence of vandalism, fighting, and drug-alcohol offenses in school was directly related to size of school." In other words, the smaller the school, the fewer the offenses.

The optional public schools tend to be significantly smaller than the standard schools. While there are few educational parks and other centers with large enrollments, the average enrollment in most optional schools would be around two hundred. If the California report is correct, this smaller size may help explain the differences in violence and vandalism that exist in optional and traditional schools.

In his recent book, *Violence in the Schools*, Michael Berger bears out this thesis by reporting that the sheer size of urban schools is a cause of violence, and that there is an "almost total lack of violence in alternative schools."

In 1976, witnesses before the U.S. Senate Subcommittee on Juvenile Delinquency recommended alternative public schools as a solution to violence and vandalism, and the Subcommittee's report endorsed this strategy.

The National Schools Public Relations Association published a special report, *Violence and Vandalism*, in which it concluded that "the single most agreed-on recommendation of educators for the resolution of school vandalism and violence — after the immediate needs of security are met — is that of offering alternatives."

Size may be a factor contributing to school absenteeism. Principals of alternative schools frequently report a lower absence rate for their students than when the latter were enrolled in larger, more conventional schools.

It is becoming increasingly clear that the solutions to juvenile vandalism and crime are not to be found in the courts and penal systems, but rather in the schools. Law enforcement, the courts, and prison are all reactive, not proactive. The addition of federal funds in the juvenile justice system has not succeeded in reducing juvenile crime. Obviously, the schools, whether conventional or alternative, have a role to play here.

A CAUTIONARY WORD

If optional public schools contribute in any way to the solutions of any of the major educational problems just cited, their development would be justified in every community. But this is by no means clear, since such matters as racial relations, segregation, crime, dishonesty, illiteracy, and absenteeism are obviously not just school problems but, rather, are issues affecting the entire educational system and the total society. It would indeed be foolish to believe that the development of a few optional schools for a few children and youth can by itself have any dramatic effect on our major social problems. And it would be equally unfair to judge optional schools solely on their ability to solve problems which the standard schools are apparently unable to solve. In short, the real justification for optional schools lies in another direction.

A Conceptual Framework for Optional Public Schools

The development of optional alternative public schools is based upon two simple ideas: 1) in a democratic society, people should have choices in all the important aspects of their lives; 2) different people learn in different ways.

Neither of these ideas is surprising. In fact, most educators and most of the general public would agree with them. What *is* surprising is that both these ideas directly conflict with the present, monolithic structure of public education, in which all children are assigned to a public school and then compelled to attend it.

THE RIGHT TO CHOOSE

In *The Soft Revolution*, Neil Postman and Charles Weingartner stated that "a major characteristic of the American culture is that it is pluralistic. If pluralism means anything, it means the availability of options. Where there are no options, you have a fraudulent pluralism — the name without the reality. This is true in business as well as in government. It is also true in education. At present, our educational system is monolithic. One has no choice but to accept the sole approach to learning offered by the schools. The situation, if not un-American, is not American in spirit."

In the 1975 report *The Adolescent, Other Citizens, and Their High Schools*, the following statement appears: "Gradually, the institution of education has moved away from the basic premise of democracy: that people should control their institutions. Education is the public institution closest to the people. Citizens have the right to be involved in governance, policy-making, and decisions affecting schools."

In the light of the above quotes, it should be made clear here that our present system of public education, which is both undemocratic and un-American, evolved by accident rather than by intent. It was natural in colonial time — perhaps even inevitable — that the colonists would import the authoritarian model of school from Western Europe. (One of the functions of this model was to screen out students who would not benefit from further schooling.) However, authoritarian schools became obsolete in 1776 when the United States became a Constitutional government.

In our early history as a nation, when a variety of schools were available for those who wanted them and could afford them, and when there was no such thing as compulsory education, no one would have imagined the eventual development of a compulsory monolithic school system. Even at the beginning of this century, in fact, many children failed to complete elementary school, and fewer than ten percent of them completed high school. Within a relatively short time, certainly less than thirty years (1920-1950), the schools, which had been previously eliminating a majority of students before they completed high school, were suddenly expected to provide secondary as well as elementary education for *all* youth. Only now are we beginning to realize that this was an impossible task. And only now are we beginning to realize that a democratic society must have an educational system that prepares its students for democratic living.

Around the country, a number of communities are beginning to offer *options* and *choice* in public education to every family at both the elementary and secondary levels (*e.g.*, Berkeley and Pasadena; Minneapolis and St. Paul; Ann Arbor and Grand Rapids; Dallas and Houston; Quincy, Illinois; Jefferson County, Colorado, etc.). When a community offers choices at every educational level, the conventional school is available by choice rather than by compulsion. This does not mean, of course, that students can choose not to attend school at all; it does mean, though, that families have a choice of schools, including the conventional school.

Recent court decisions have dealt with this matter of choice in public education. The U.S. Third Circuit Court of Appeals, for example, ruled that a girl should not be admitted to Philadelphia's prestigious Central High School, a 140-year-old high school for academically talented males, because she could get a comparably good education at the Philadelphia High School for Girls. The Court went on to state that "if she were to prevail, then all single-sex schools would have to be abolished...and parents who prefer an education in a public single-sex school would be denied their freedom of choice." Whether there should be single-sex alternative public schools is a separate issue. However, the court's recognition of parents' freedom of choice in public education is significant here.

In *Wisconsin v. Yoder*, the U.S. Supreme Court ended compulsory secondary education for Amish youth. The Court's decision contained the following statement: "The high school tends to emphasize intellectual and scientific accomplishments, self-distinction, competitiveness, worldy success, and social life with other students. Amish society emphasizes informal learning-through-doing; a life of 'goodness' rather than a life of intellect; wisdom, rather than technical knowledge; community welfare rather than competition..." Clearly, there may be parents, other than the Amish, who would prefer cooperation and community welfare to competition and self-distinction, and who would also prefer that their children gain wisdom rather than technical knowledge.

Both parents and teachers are seeking today a greater voice in public education. And more choice means more voice for both groups, though they have not realized this yet. Usually, when one group gets more power, another group gets less. Not in this case, however. The people who originally decided that everyone should be compelled to attend one school aren't around any longer. So, giving parents a choice in their children's schools and giving teachers a choice in the schools they'll teach in provides more power for both.

THE RIGHT TO LEARN

Different children learn in different ways and at different times; the same child learns in different ways at different stages of development. Most psychologists, educators, and informed laypersons would accept these two statements. But,

ever since the demise of the one-room school, the public schools have typically taught all children in the same way at the same time. Until recently, uniformity of schools was assumed to be equal educational opportunity. Only today are we beginning to recognize that a school which expects all children to learn in the same way and at the same time is in fact a violation of equal educational opportunity.

Though many children learn well in the standard public school with its emphasis on academic talent and cognitive skills, others learn better in the less structured environment of the open school (with learning centers rather than the academic classroom). Still others learn best in an individualized, continuous progress school, where each student progresses at his own pace. And there are those, too, who perform particularly well in schools based on the learning principles of Maria Montessori, of Jean Piaget, or of behavioral modification.

The psychology of education — the study of how people learn — is less than a century old. Complete theories of learning and corresponding theories of instruction are still to be developed. What we *do* know today is that some children learn well in one setting, while others learn well in another. Why then should we not be providing, on a far greater scale, different settings to meet the learning needs of different children? Is this not what equality of educational opportunity is all about — providing the conditions for the optimal learning of each child?

At a time when there is much concern over declining test scores and the need for the development of basic skills, some parents may feel that the standard school is the one that is best equipped to handle such problems. This is not necessarily true, though. What isn't always common knowledge is the fact that all of the alternative schools are attempting to develop the basic skills, even though they may be using different methodologies. In some cases, as a matter of fact, alternative schools have been highly successful in developing the basic skills of students who were not doing well in the standard schools.

In this connection, Ronald Santora and Louise Jensen wrote in 1974 in the *English Journal* that:

> "*Students themselves are not the cause of reading failure.* All people possess the strong language competence and rich experiential background necessary to master reading. While some of the causes of reading failure are surely psychological, we wish to posit emphatically that reading failure is not caused by children who have been labeled as 'defective' in some cognitive sense or 'deficient' in some linguistic sense. If failure has occurred, it is most often the failure of the schools themselves, their environments, attitudes and methods of instruction, or all three. It is the schools that must attempt to restructure themselves in order to accommodate a *linguistic and cultural pluralism* among those they serve. If this sounds like a plea for alternative learning environments, *it is*."

As long as all the children in a community are assigned to one school, they will be expected to conform to the demands that school makes upon them. Those who are unable to conform will have problems. Schools have always labeled those youngsters who somehow fail to learn in a standard setting as slow, hyperactive, disruptive, emotionally disturbed, etc. This labeling clearly blames the victim, rather than the school, for the failure to learn.

Recently, this tendency toward labeling has taken a particularly disturbing turn. Under the guise of treating "learning disabilities," schools have been drugging children who do not conform to the school to which they are assigned as a way to "improve" their behavior. Estimates of the number of elementary school children currently on drugs that are prescribed to control hyperactivity in the classroom vary from one to six million, or from about one in thirty children to about one in five. And this, despite a British medical study that found that hyperactivity was a "decidedly uncommon disorder" affecting only the rare individual (about one of two thousand).

In "Learning Disabilities: Education's Newest Growth Industry," Schrag and Divoky have reported that this form of disability is increasingly affecting "primarily white, middle-class children." As one instance of this, they mention a case where parents received a note from the school nurse that their son was hyperactive. Therefore, they promptly sent the child to another school, and the problem never surfaced again.

We know of another very similar instance where parents, unwilling to subject their child to drugs, requested that she be allowed to attend an alternative elementary school instead. Placed in an alternative program (an environmental school with much outdoor learning and with projects, instead of academic work), the girl showed no signs of hyperactivity. On the contrary, she was quiet and cooperative, and displayed a high degree of artistic talent that she had not previously shown in the standard classroom. While these two instances hardly merit a generalization, they suggest the need for exploring further the possible merits of sending students who are "learning disabled" to alternative learning environments.

In Taft, California, a class action suit was recently brought against the school district, charging the school authorities with having coerced children into taking the psychoactive drug *Ritalin* as a condition for attending school. The suit also charged that the children were then placed in classes for the mentally retarded, *without* the knowledge or consent of their parents.

None of the above is meant to suggest that some children are not in need of medication to help them learn. *But* we must question the practice of assigning children to one classroom and then labeling them as "learning disabled" if they cannot adjust to it. In our view, the optional schools provide a means of adjusting the school system to the students, rather than forcing them to adjust to the school.

Optional Schools: What Are The Problems?

In spite of the widespread support for optional public schools, there exists nonetheless an ambivalent attitude toward alternatives among many educators and lay people. Although they recognize that the standard schools are not meeting the needs of all students, they are still reluctant to endorse the development of alternative schools and programs that would compete for increasingly difficult-to-get tax dollars.

Furthermore, alternatives in their view must be alternatives to something, and that something is usually well established by tradition. Loyalty to the traditional creates a natural resistance among institutions as well as individuals. In fact, the larger the bureaucratic institution, the greater its resistance to change.

In spite of the moderately widespread publicity about alternative schools in both professional and popular publications, the concept is not yet familiar to the majority of our citizens. And, since many people tend to favor the familiar over the unfamiliar, the dissemination of such information on optional schools is a continuing need.

In some communities, there is a stigma on the alternative school. Because some vocational schools and career education centers have been dumping grounds in the past, because some alternative schools are designed for dropouts and pregnant girls, and because in some communities disruptive students are being assigned (without choice) to "alternative schools," many parents have become convinced that alternative schools are for other people's children, not for their own. Still others have a preconceived notion of an alternative school. Because they are familiar with the free school concept, they mistakenly believe that all alternative schools provide unlimited freedom and little learning or teaching.

Sometimes, alternative schools are established prematurely without adequate dialogue and understanding on the part of the parents, students, and teachers who are to be involved. Sometimes, too, an enthusiastic administrator or board member attempts to start an alternative school without sufficiently analyzing local needs. Or a vested interest group within the community may try to force the board and/or the administration to establish an alternative school without even assessing needs and acceptability. And faddism can also be a problem. Just because one community has a successful alternative is no reason for other communities to copy it.

Over-enthusiasm can be a problem, too. In every community there seem to be a few teachers, students, and parents who want to flee from the conventional school. They know what they are fleeing *from,* but they do not analyze or care about what they are fleeing *to.* Often, they may have very different and conflicting views on what an alternative school should be.

Providing adequate time for planning and staff development should be an important concern. While planning time is clearly desirable when a new school is opened, it is absolutely critical in the case of an alternative school.

The same is true in terms of providing adequate information to prospective students and their parents, since the decisions they make should be based on sound, intelligent judgment.

Since the first alternative school in any community will be a novelty, it can well attract undue attention from the media and from visitors outside the community. If the necessary steps to curb this aren't taken, this can easily become a problem.

Evaluation is usually the first problem mentioned when the staffs of alternative schools get together. This problem is generally caused by a lack of adequate planning.

Since most alternative public schools operate on the same per capita budget as conventional schools, they will usually have some start-up expenses just as a new conventional school would have on opening. So funding, or the lack of it, can be a real problem.

In addition to these implementation problems, there are a host of operational problems as well — marking and grading practices, record-keeping procedures, credit, transcripts and college admissions, accreditation, building codes, fire, safety, health regulations, and transportation arrangements.

Finally, most alternative schools are frequently oversubscribed, and there is a long waiting list to get in. The result is considerable resentment on the part of those not admitted. To combat this problem, each alternative school must develop fair and equitable admission procedures.

Optional Schools: What Are The Results?

It is probably too early yet to assess the successes and failures of optional alternative public schools. To date, few such schools have failed in the sense that they have actually closed their doors. And, as for those schools that appear to be in danger of closing, they generally have relied heavily on outside funding for their routine operation and/or were started without adequate dialogue and support within their community.

The fact that there is little research to date to verify either success or failure is not unusual. We haven't much research to verify the success or failure of conventional schools, either. If anything, most of the alternative public schools have had more comprehensive evaluations than conventional schools. And, while a single evaluation rarely makes a case for generalization, cumulative alternative school evaluations which exist do suggest certain tentative conclusions.

Both students and teachers report that the optional schools tend to be more "humane" than the conventional secondary school that they attended or taught in. At least part of this feeling is attributable to the smaller size of the alternative school (as mentioned earlier, most alternative schools have fewer than 200 students), and the fact that most of these teachers and students have come from schools with an enrollment of more than a thousand students. Certainly, a school for several thousand is likely to have more rules and constraints and be more impersonal than a school for two hundred, and so be perceived as less "humane."

Many teachers and administrators report that students and their parents tend to be more loyal to, and more cooperative with, a school they themselves have chosen. They also report a preference for working with a student population that is voluntary, rather than compulsory.

In cases where alternative schools have been in operation for a few years, there is usually a long waiting list of applicants. In some communities, in fact, hundreds and even thousands of students apply for alternative schools each year, indicating a real community acceptance of the optional school.

Most alternative public schools have been subjected to some form of tion, usually similar to those used in the conventional schools of the same district.

How do the students who attend alternative schools generally fare? According to a 1974 Ford Foundation report, "where standard measures of achievement such as test scores and college admissions are applicable, they show that alternative school students perform at least as well as their counterparts in traditional school programs, and usually better. Attendance rates almost without exception exceed those in regular schools."

Most alternative high schools send a higher percentage of their graduates on to college than do the regular high schools within the same district. After Parkway's first two classes had graduated, for example, John Bremer (then the director) reported that "every student who had applied to college had been accepted, most of them by their first choice."

Finally, whether the factors involved are humaneness, size, or physical environment, the principals of alternative high schools report that there is less absence, less truancy, and less vandalism than in their conventional high school counterparts. This alone speaks well of alternative schools and of their future role in American education.

The Dallas Story

9

The Dallas Story

WILLIAM M. TAYLOR, JR.

Introduction

Judge William M. Taylor Jr. presents the history of desegregation efforts in Dallas since the 1960's. His emphasis, however, is on the role the community played in making the order he issued as successful as it has become—particularly, with respect to the Dallas Magnets. Judge Taylor also discusses here the rationale for the order, both from a legal and personal point of view.

It is truly a pleasure for me to be invited to participate in this First Annual International Conference on Magnet Schools. I am honored to be among so many dedicated and well-known educators and others interested in education. And I am particularly pleased to have the opportunity to relate the story of Magnet Schools in Dallas.

Let me begin by pointing out that, contrary to popular belief, federal judges do not particularly enjoy telling school people how to run their business. And that certainly is not my intention today. There are many fine educators, businessmen, and citizens of this town who could probably do a much better job of describing the Dallas experience, as well as of offering specific recommendations, than I can. As a matter of fact, the Dallas School System started telling me many years ago exactly how to conduct *my* business.

Nonetheless, I would like to review here where we have been in Dallas, in the hope that you might pick up a few ideas. And I would also like to take a look at the Magnet School concept as a legal remedy for segregated schools. This doesn't mean, though, that I come today prepared to offer panaceas, desegregation-wise or education-wise, and I hope that no one goes home saying that some judge in Texas claimed that if we were to do it this way, or that way, we would revolutionize education and meet the legal requirements for desegregation.

Rather, you can say that Mac Taylor truly believes that the Magnet School concept is working for Dallas. And that, based on his experience, he believes Magnet Schools can provide not only a voluntary vehicle for desegregating schools, but also forward-looking and exciting educational opportunities.

Every time I get the opportunity to talk about our Dallas experiences, I am reminded of the ten-year-old boy who, when he came home from Sunday School, was asked by his mother what he had learned. "Well," said the boy, "our teacher told us about how God sent Moses behind the enemy lines to rescue the Israelites from the Egyptians. He brought them to the Red Sea, and then Moses ordered the engineers to build a pontoon bridge. After they had all crossed over, the Israelites looked back and saw the Egyptian tanks coming. Quick as a flash, Moses grabbed his walkie-talkie and asked the Air Force to send bombers to blow up the bridge and save the Israelites." "Bobby!" exclaimed his mother. "Is that really the way the teacher told the story?" "Well, not exactly," Bobby admitted. "But if I told it *her* way, you'd never believe it."

Well, sometimes I feel that's the way people from other cities are going to think when I start telling them about how this community has rallied in support of the Dallas schools and their efforts to implement school desegregation, but particularly in support of Magnet Schools. I know they are not going to believe it, because it has not happened this way before in any other community I know of in the nation.

But it was not always thus. So I would like to return to the past and to provide you with a little background leading up to today's Dallas Magnet story.

Dallas, like many southern cities, has been involved in one form of desegregation or another for a number of years now. The *Brown Decision* of 1954, of course, struck down the separate-but-equal concept, which was included as part of state law here in Texas. In the early 1960's, the Dallas schools began adopting the neighborhood concept in a year-by-year, stair-step fashion. This process was soon speeded up by the federal courts and, by the late 60's, all Dallas schools at all levels were operating as neighborhood schools.

Because of housing patterns, however, many schools were still racially segregated. In October 1970, I became personally involved in this area of concern when a multi-ethnic group of citizens, on behalf of their children, filed a class action suit seeking legal relief under the Fourteenth Amendment for what they considered to be segregated schools. After months of hearings and the submission of many plans by the school system, the plaintiffs, and outside experts, I issued an order in August 1971. The order called for the transportation of students at the secondary level, and a somewhat more creative approach at the elementary level, involving the pairing of schools and actual classrooms via field trips, social activities, and television.

The latter portion of my order was immediately appealed by the plaintiffs, and stayed (not approved for immediate implementation) by the Fifth Circuit Court of Appeals in New Orleans. Meanwhile, when the schools opened in September, some 6,000 Junior and Senior High students boarded the buses, and the Dallas system began implementation of a plan which would last for some four years, or until we again heard from the Court of Appeals.

In July of 1975, the Fifth Circuit sent my original order back, along with some broad guidelines for developing a new plan for Dallas schools. Accordingly, hearings began again for the district attorneys, the plaintiffs, as well as a number of interveners in the case. By this time, as you can imagine, I was somewhat concerned about finding a solution that would be acceptable to the community, as well as to the Court of Appeals. As a long-time resident of this city—having lived here since I was four years of age—I obviously wanted to do what was best for Dallas. On the other hand, I fully understood my legal responsibilities, and was very much aware of the responsibility my colleagues in New Orleans had for seeing that I carried out my job.

I would be less that candid if I did not admit that, during these early years of busing in Dallas, I was somewhat disappointed and concerned about the lack of commitment toward carrying out the orders of the court. Now don't misinterpret that to mean that people were not obeying the law of the land, for they were. But there was a great lack of enthusiasm, to say the least. And leadership, particularly from the business community, was nowhere to be found.

Accordingly, in the fall of 1975, I proceeded to blast everyone in sight for his or her lack of commitment, involvement, and leadership. For, you see, I believe in this city; believe that Dallas has the resources, the ability, and the vision to do anything it wants to do, if it has the will to do it. And, fortunately, Dallas did not fail me or itself. For, at about this time, the leadership hibernation ended: civic, business, and governmental leaders now came forth to call for positive action and to offer assistance and resources which would ensure that whatever plan we came up with would be enthusiastically and sincerely supported.

In late 1975, I called together all the litigants to inform them that I had asked the Dallas Chamber of Commerce's Alliance Education Task Force to participate in the hearings as a friend of the court. This multi-ethnic group had gone out and obtained a private grant to help develop a desegregation plan, and had been working for some four and one-half months visiting other cities and school districts, looking for new and creative ways to help desegregate the school system, as well as to improve the quality of education. Naturally, I saw the Alliance Task Force as an ideal vehicle for compromise.

It was my thinking that a group of citizens with a multi-ethnic composition could come up with a plan that would be acceptable both to the community and to the main actors in the suit. And so, in early 1976, when the Alliance came in with a new concept for desegregating Dallas schools, I accepted its plan and ordered the school district to work out the details for its implementation. The new plan involved much more than merely student assignment; in effect, it was a total educational plan, one which reorganized the school system and placed great emphasis on instructional strategies and community participation.

The plan standardized grade arrangements on a district-wide basis—establishing early childhood centers in grades K-3; intermediate schools for grades 4-6; middle schools for grades 7-8; and four-year high schools for grades 9-12. This approach was designed to enhance instruction and speed up desegregation.

Instructionally, the configuration was in line with the district's revamping of its entire program of learning—something school officials had been working on for several years, and something I certainly wanted to build on. Desegregationally, this structure made it possible for us to provide systematic remedies on a district-wide basis. K-3 students were to stay in their neighborhood schools, where we expected reduced adult-pupil ratios and massive community involvement. Transportation was to take place at the intermediate and middle school levels—in areas which were not naturally integrated. Six sub-districts were also set up under the plan, with three of them being left completely alone as far as transportation was concerned. Two of these were considered to be naturally integrated, while the last one (which remains even today almost totally black) received special programs and staffing.

As for the high school level, the Magnet School concept was the main desegregation tool. While many students participated in various other voluntary transfer programs, we placed our faith in the ability of these special schools to carry the load of encouraging integration. And we have been rewarded, I may add, beyond our fondest expectations.

Since many of you toured Dallas Magnet Schools only yesterday, I am sure you are somewhat familiar with the details. But, for those of you who are not, let me point out that the Dallas Plan calls for the use of Magnet-type programs at three different levels. At the intermediate grade level, the programs are known as Vanguard Schools, with each specializing in a particular programmatic area. For example, Dallas Vanguards include a program for the talented and gifted, a fundamental school, a center for individually guided education, a special communications school, and even a Montessori program—the only one that I know of in a public school system in this country. [*Cincinnati is credited by the American Montessori Society with having the first Montessori school in a public school setting. It, in fact, opened one year before the Dallas school. Dallas's program, though, is the first public Montessori school in the nation to serve grades 4-6.* EDITOR'S NOTE]

At the middle school level, the Magnets are known as Academies. And, during the initial year of the plan, three of them were set up to focus on the areas of ecology, career exploration, and the classics. These have been exciting programs, offering parents and students alternative educational opportunities while moving toward a desegregated setting. The school district is now working on plans to expand the Academies in order to provide a feeder system for students who have been enrolled in the Vanguard Schools.

But the most exciting aspect of the Magnet School program is, of course, at the high school level. Dallas began the school year with four Magnet programs—in the arts, health careers, business and management, and transportation. The original goal was to attract at least four to five hundred students to each of these schools. More than 4,000 students are now enrolled, and plans are on the drawing boards for the addition of two new Magnets next year—one in law and public administration, the other in the area of human services. Several other new Magnet Schools, including one in math-science technology, are also in the works and will, in fact, be housed in newly constructed facilities in the near future.

Our community has been turned on and excited by the Magnet School concept—particularly, the high school Magnets. One of the prime reasons for this is that the schools are built upon the successful model the district developed in its Skyline Career Center. These programs have proven track records of providing students with important skills to market, as well as a background for advanced and higher learning, if that is what they desire.

The key to all this, of course, is the commitment and support of the community—and that we have had here amply. Early on, in fact, when the plan was first adopted, the Dallas business community came forward and provided top businessmen and other leaders in their field to help in the establishment of these schools. The business leadership also got involved in the recruitment of students, providing resources to help in the marketing campaign, and finding people to participate in the selling job. The business community continues its commitment by providing jobs and work experiences for students in each of the Magnet programs. Businessmen serve as tutors, advisors, planners, and friends of students. To me, it is the most exciting thing I have seen in education in years. And not only have Dallas parents and students been turned on, but I am aware that students from suburban school districts are now enrolling in, and inquiring about enrollment in, Magnet programs.

Based upon the Dallas experience, I would say that the Magnet School Story is just beginning, and that the future is very bright. As you can plainly see, the entire Dallas Plan was built around and hinges upon the success of Magnet-type programs. As a federal judge, I have always been convinced that desegregation would work *only* if we found new and creative alternatives to massive transportation. And I think that past major court decisions, including *Swann,* call for that. To me, Magnet Schools provide one of those creative alternatives. They are not only legitimate and proven desegregation tools, but they also appear to be the wave of the future in terms of public education.

I am fully convinced that the problems of public education cannot be separated from the problems of society in general. If schools are going to succeed, new linkages have to be created with the community at large. And, if the community is going to prosper and grow, the community's leadership has to provide the resources and support to ensure quality public education for its citizens.

Obviously, whether one talks about Dallas or any other city in this country, our society and schools will not survive without new partnerships being developed. Magnet Schools, and public education in general, depend upon the full cooperation of school officials, community leaders, and businessmen in the planning, implementation, and evaluation of all programs. This, of course, calls for flexibility among educators, full support and commitment from the community leadership, and use of the resources and expertise that businessmen can provide.

None of this is easy. I say that based upon our experience here. But, in the long run, everyone benefits. Such cooperation makes the educator's job much easier and it provides the community with good schools and superior educational opportunities. It also assures businessmen, who certainly have an interest in a strong community, of a sound economic base if they help make sure that the schools are strong and that jobs are available for qualified job applicants.

Perhaps the following little story about the merits of cooperation puts all of this into proper perspective. One night a house caught fire. The fire spread rapidly to other houses. Each family ran frantically about, attempting to save its individual possessions. A wise bystander, noticing this, remarked: "You are silly, selfish people. Instead of each one trying to save his own possessions, why don't you all get together and put out the fire, so that it will not spread any further?"

If you leave here today with any one message, that is the one I would like you to take away. Our society is far too complex, and the problems we face too massive, for individual institutions to face alone. *If democracy, as we know it, is to survive, institutions must work together to see that it does.* I know it can be done, because I have seen it happen here in Dallas.

An Epilogue:
Alternative Schools: Who Needs Them?

DR. DONALD R. WALDRIP

Introduction

Following the First Annual International Conference on Magnet Schools, Dr. Donald R. Waldrip appeared some two weeks later as an ''Invited Lecturer'' at the annual meeting of the National School Boards Association. This meeting was held at Houston, Texas, from March 26 to 29, 1977. Since Dr. Waldrip drew extensively from the papers presented at the Dallas conference, in making this presentation, and since it summarizes many of the positions offered in the preceding pages of this book, it appears here as a conclusion.

Last year a large-city superintendent of schools died. To his surprise, he did not go to heaven. To his even greater surprise, he was in hell for two weeks before he realized he wasn't in his office.

Dr. Nolan Estes, General Superintendent of the Dallas Independent School District, reported about three years ago that the average tenure of the large-city superintendent was 2.8 years. Some of these outstanding educators who took only a fleeting glimpse at superintending see little hope for our nation's schools and cities. They see everyone fighting and no one discussing education and children. They see pressure groups determining long-term policy, bureaucracies sleeping through rapid changes in school board composition and administrative leadership, and various segments of the education profession taking adversary positions on insubstantial issues, rather than cooperating to address the substantive ones.

In 1918, in his poem, ''The Second Coming,'' W.B. Yeats predicted the collapse of our ''scientific, democratic, fact-accumulative, heterogeneous civilization.''

> Turning and turning in the widening gyre
> The falcon cannot hear the falconer;
> Things fall apart; the centre cannot hold;
> Mere anarchy is loosed upon the world,
> The blood-dimmed tide is loosed, and everywhere
> The ceremony of innocence is drowned;
> The best lack all conviction, while the worst
> Are full of passionate intensity.

In the second verse, Yeats goes on to predict that ''surely some revelation is at hand.'' However, those educators who have given up on urban education do not perceive this imminent revelation. Instead, they feel only the disequilibrium. They see only the anarchy, the drowning innocence; the apathy of the best and the intense hatred of the worst.[1] Are they correct in their assessment? Do their feelings accurately describe urban education — its present and its future?

If *I* subscribed to these doom-laden predictions, my optimistic ancestors would disown me. I was taught to believe — not merely to act as if I believed — that all things turn out ultimately for the best. I, therefore, choose to believe that those who say urban education is doomed have failed to grasp the knowledge that comes from conflict, the beauty of change, the hope that springs from new experience.

Why, even today, three years after Dr. Estes' report on the tenure of superintendents, Dr. Paul Salmon, Executive Director of the American Association of School Administrators, reports that the average time in office for these beleaguered souls is now closer to five years than to three. Hope springs eternal!

Why, in the face of all evidence to the contrary, do I see (if you will pardon the expression) light at the end of the tunnel? All of those citizens who have recently moved from our major cities to the suburbs or who have, within the past few years, sought the haven of private or parochial education for their children do not, I am sure, see that light. Instead, they see an endlessly dark tunnel, or else one that is hopelessly clogged with teacher strikes, school board politics, angry parents, disruptive students, and bankrupt budgets.

I don't. I see students who were once disruptive, but who are not anymore; I see teachers who once posed as adversaries to the system, now happy and productive; I see parents who had almost made their disgust with the system a vocation, now the biggest boosters of public education. What caused this turnabout? In a word: alternatives.

Just what is an alternative school? An alternative school is one with which parents, students, and teachers become associated, voluntarily. No one need be a part of an alternative school unless he or she wants to. But alternative to what? And that answer has to be, an alternative to the school to which a student or teacher is normally assigned.

School-aged children residing within a district who do not attend a private or parochial school define the enrolled population which the district must serve. Geographic attendance areas determine who will attend what school. The establishment of a common curriculum has guaranteed equality of educational opportunity within public education. Since parents, once having established a place of residence, are usually unable to select the public school their children will attend, boards of education have attempted to ensure that the quality of education is equal — not necessarily good, but equal — throughout the district. Equality of educational opportunity has, therefore, found expression in a common curriculum and common instructional methods.[2]

"For years educators have disagreed about the one best method of educating youngsters. We have also argued about what should be taught and, in the context of the traditional grade structure, when. In fact, many — including the speaker —

have spent a great amount of time attempting to eliminate the traditional grade structure.''[3]

Many of you will remember the days when all ''progressive'' educators were advocating modular scheduling, team teaching, and continuous progress education (otherwise known as the upgraded school). ''Advocates of these methodologies contributed greatly to the re-examination of our conventional lock-step educational system, and they were absolutely right in their conclusions — for a great number of students. Many children do function more productively in more open-ended, flexible settings, but even these environmental paragons did not serve all students well.''[4]

Though some children learn more effectively in a highly structured environment, the admission that no one best method exists for educating all children was the beginning of the alternative school movement. We educators have proclaimed for years that children have different needs, aspirations, and even learning styles, but, until the advent of the alternative school, we had expected all of these differences to be addressed by a single classroom teacher — or, at most, a ''team'' of two or three teachers.

Mario Fantini, Dean of the University of Massachusetts, has perhaps said it best:

> We say that diversity is a basic belief of our way of life; we say that people are entitled to their points of view whether conservative or liberal; we say that each person is entitled to a choice. Yet these principles are not applied to the public schools. Instead, we have been looking for the *one* best way of doing things that will please everyone. Putting all of our eggs in one basket has not been a good practice. Forcing all learners and their families to adjust to a single school model has posed a severe strain on both. The normative school has not prepared for the wide range of human variability that converged on it and increasing numbers of learners could not connect with the scholastic diet being served. The result is growing frustration on both sides. This leads to disconnection, discontent and confrontation.[5]

Fantini goes on to say that too often our schools have just switched

> from one orthodoxy to another — often without parent, student or teacher choice....At times, tugs-of-war were initiated with groups vying for one form to dominate another. School board members were elected to ''push for'' one form of schooling; e.g. fundamental, open. Sometimes four to three school board ''majorities'' establish policies that move the schools in one direction or another. Obviously, mandating one pattern on a diverse community is bound to elicit controversy and dissatisfaction.

> It is this so-called inflexibility and unresponsiveness to the sentiments of the educational consumers that is behind the alternative school movement on a political level. If one is an educational conservative or liberal, one has the right to a legitimate form of education that is compatible.[6]

The basis of this new relationship is best expressed by two interdependent elements: choice and options. Alternative education, in whatever form it assumes, must allow for real parent/student choice through the creation of a number of educational options. These optional public schools take many different forms and may be classified in many different ways. They may be classified, for example, according to their modes of instruction — *i.e.*, as free schools, open schools, fundamental schools, continuous progress schools, behavior modification schools, Individually Guided Education (IGE) Schools, and Montessori Schools. Or they may be classified on the basis of instructional emphasis — *i.e.*, as creative and performing arts schools, environmental schools, multicultural schools, bilingual schools, and math-science schools. Alternative schools may also focus on resources, usually those that cannot be provided in every school. Examples of this would include schools-without-walls (or citywide schools), learning centers, career centers, and educational parks. Finally, alternative schools may best serve the needs of a highly diversified clientele, and would include such settings as dropout centers, street academies, evening schools, and pregnancy-maternity centers.[7] One may see from the classifications just enumerated that combinations of these would be feasible in many settings, and that many possibilities were not even mentioned. But once a student or teacher is *assigned* to any one of the above categories, it ceases to be an alternative. Teachers *apply* to teach in alternative schools; students *voluntarily* attend them.

In Cincinnati, classifications depend on whether the school building is emptied of students to make room for a new student body in a newly created alternative, whether the alternative program occupies only a portion of a school building, or whether a neighborhood school, serving its own students first, is converted into an alternative offering.

Yet, for all these differences in classification, the one constant among all alternative schools is a concern for the development of basic skills among the student body. Regardless of the nature or structure of the alternative, it must be deeply concerned with reading, writing, and arithmetic. If it does not pay attention to these curricular areas, it is a hoax and should be treated as such.

In fact, ''alternative schools combine the best of both conservative and liberal philosophies of education. They are conservative in that they conserve the best of traditional education: emphasis on basic skills and academic achievement. They are liberal in their assumption that parents and their children know best what their educational needs and interests are.''[8]

Before a school district can formally initiate alternative school programs, it must define for itself its level of commitment to this kind of education as well as its specific objectives. Since the change to alternative programs requires that the system undertake a fundamentally unique enterprise, district administrators and parents had better have a good idea of just what they are seeking to accomplish, and the extent to which they are willing — and able — to support such programs. For example, a parent's willingness to enroll his or her children in an alternative school signifies a long-term commitment to this type of schooling. Yet if this is a big decision for a parent, it is even more so for the district itself. Like all education today, alternative education is susceptible to the often unpredictable dynamics of the market place and the whims of politicians. So a district's commitment to alternative education and to developing and sustaining new programs should be in direct proportion to the enthusiasm and support of its parent/student constituency. But it must go even further. The school system cannot merely create programs and expect them to succeed. The board and the superintendent should decide which goals will best serve the community and then proceed to develop the kind of program marketing and student recruitment system that will ensure success.

The five goals which are most often attained by a well-developed system of alternatives are:

1. improvement of the quality of instruction throughout the school system
2. a creative response to identifiable interest groups who are seeking changes within the system that other groups may oppose
3. better service for students of varying interests, aptitudes, and aspirations
4. reduction in racial isolation within the school system through voluntary means
5. maintenance of a middle-income constituency in the city.

Let us examine each of the above in more detail — *first, the quality of instruction throughout the school system*. I have three children. They live under the same roof, eat the same food, have the same parents. Yet their educational needs are entirely different. My first child, a daughter, operates best in a flexible arrangement. Rigidity bores her to death; she likes variety, and can shift from one setting to another with ease. She would profit from attending a school that offers her many options, different-sized classes, and time to reflect. During her early school years, an IGE or continuous progress elementary school would have been ideal for her. During her early teens, a modularly scheduled, phase-elective secondary school emphasizing the humanities would have suited her perfectly. Though she is in college now, rarely during her twelve years of public education did she have the right setting for her. A few times of course she did, and, because of her optimistic nature, those are the times she remembers.

My second child, and my first son, is different. His ambition is to become middle linebacker on the Green Bay Packers. He is reserved; he needs structure. In fact, he cannot function well in school without quite a bit of structure. He is an excellent tenth-grade student, studies hard, and is dedicated to being the best at whatever he does. He is the only person I know who watches television, talks on the phone, reads Latin, and lifts weights — all at the same time. That, my friends, takes organization.

He is lucky, though. He attends an alternative school — a college preparatory (highly structured) alternative school. He studies about four hours a night — takes after his mother that way.

My third child — my second son — is different from the first two. He is so independent that I am sometimes afraid he will not live to adulthood. He is a seventh grader, and has already been mugged twice; still, he loves all people and animals, and is sure they love him. (And, usually, he is right.) He is constantly bruised — from the top of his head to the soles of his feet. His legs are blue from trying something new on his bicycle and not quite perfecting it the first twenty tries. Oh, yes, one thing I forgot to tell you; he also plays the fiddle. And he plays the fiddle pretty darn well.

When we lived in Dallas, we sent both our sons across town to a school that had some black kids in it. (Since my daughter's school was already integrated, she went closer to home.) You see, we wanted our children to have an integrated education, as did the parents of thirty-three other children who, together with our two, attended the same church. Each morning these thirty-five youngsters would meet at the church to board a bus for a forty-five minute trip to a school serving about nine-hundred black children. This school had a program called Suzuki Violin, and my younger son entered the class as a second grader.

When we moved to Cincinnati, he naturally wanted to continue playing the violin. So we found him a private teacher, and he progressed nicely. Strangely, though, he hated music at his new school. He made all "O's" (outstanding achievement) in everything but music. In this subject, he consistently received an "N," which stands for "needs improvement." He refused to sing in class and, when his mother and I conferred with him about this, he said, "I won't sing. I can't stand those dumb songs."

One day, teachers all over the city went on strike: Tim's neighborhood school was practically inoperative. After a few days I decided to take him to visit a few of the schools which were still in operation: namely, the alternative schools. The first one he saw was the School for Creative and Performing Arts. He hasn't left it yet. That summer, he took his one-quarter-sized violin, and went to audition for the school. He was accepted not only in violin classes, but also in drama and vocal music. *Vocal music*? We were stunned. The kid hated to sing — he had told us so himself. Yet his first year there, he was selected for All-City Boychoir. The following year, he sang the soprano solo in Vivaldi's "Gloria." Soon after, he sang the lead in a Benjamin Britten opera with the Cincinnati Symphony Orchestra. The next thing I knew, a man from New York had heard him sing and Tim was being called to New York to audition for this and that. This past year he sang several professional roles, among them that of "Oliver" in the musical by the same name which ran for five weeks in Cincinnati's professional theater, Playhouse in the Park. Next month he opens at the Uris Theater on Broadway in New York, where he will sing the role of a young prince and act as understudy for Louis (son of Anna) in "The King and I," starring Yul Brynner and Constance Towers. In fact, Brynner and Richard Rodgers selected him themselves.

This kid is only twelve years old. Perhaps as many as twenty other children in his school could tell similar stories. One of them I know sang at Carnegie Hall. Another toured with the Metropolitan Opera Company. Still another performed in a Walt Disney production of "Peter Pan." Five or six of them have been on MGM Children's Specials, broadcast on NBC-TV. Three more have been on Broadway during the past two years. Producers looking for young talent now come to Cincinnati's School for Creative and Performing Arts first. Yet none of these children — including my son — would have been able to develop their obvious talents in their traditional neighborhood schools. The alternative school has already given them great experience and helped develop their talents, and this may someday give them a big jump ahead in their careers. But don't get me wrong; the school is not a "Shirley Temple factory." The child lead in Richard Rodgers's *Rex* returned to the school in Cincinnati after having performed on Broadway, only to sing in the chorus in the school's production of *Carnival*. He did not have the leading part. In this school, the leads are passed around, so that everyone gets to be a "star" — if only for a night. And so, my son, who was making "N's" and who refused to sing "those dumb songs" in his neighborhood school, will, after three years in an alternative school, soon make his debut on Broadway. This has to be some kind of success story, and all because the right alternative school was available at the right time for a kid whose particular needs were not being met by his neighborhood school. Oh, by the way, in case you were wondering — the kid can read, write, and compute, too. The school places great emphasis on these basics — so much so that the staff will not allow a student to perform onstage or to show art work in an exhibit if his or her academic work is not up to standards.

Why have I gone into all this? Because, if my three children are so different from one another in their character and needs, just think how different the children of a total school district are — or even the children of a single school. To improve the quality of instruction in any system, large or small, one must match the learning styles of the children to appropriate learning environments. *All* districts should have alternatives; *no* school or school district is too large or too small. New York and Los Angeles have alternatives, but so does Quincy, Illinois; Northeast San Antonio; Pasadena, California; and Richardson, Texas.

The second goal of alternatives is to respond creatively to identifiable interest groups who are seeking changes within the system that other groups may oppose. School board members and superintendents, in particular, must remember that those groups who demand fundamental education or back-to-basics, as well as the groups who demand that we "de-school" society, are not necessarily wrong. In fact, for some students, they are quite right. Why have certain students left public education for private schools? Why have some creative teachers left the public classroom to form their own schools? Is it because such schools are better? Yes and no. Better for some, but not for all.

My position is that there should be no reason why a child has to attend a private school. (Attending parochial schools for religious reasons is another matter.) If the public schools offered adequate alternatives, and if they met the needs of all identifiable interest groups, they clearly would be adequate to meet all educational needs except religious ones.

When I first arrived in Cincinnati, I found that several public school teachers had resigned to form their own secondary school, something called the "New Morning School." This school treated the entire city as a classroom. Much like the Parkway Program in Philadelphia, the New Morning School had its students work on farms, in hospitals, at the universities, in banks, and at any number of other places. At the same time, these students still studied English, history, science and math; only their elective credits were earned *outside* the classroom. As a result, I found that some of them really knew what was happening at City Hall; others actually knew what occurred behind stage at the theater, and still others knew more about banking than the Superintendent of Schools did.

The alternative program, entitled "Citywide Learning Community," was the easiest one that I ever organized. I merely hired the entire New Morning staff, and they brought their students with them. That school met a need that the public sector should have been meeting. Today it does, even though it doesn't yet meet the needs of all high school students — only about 200 of them. Certainly, though, many of its present students who could never afford a private school are now receiving an equivalent education.

Goal number three is to better serve students of varying interests, aptitudes, and aspirations. This goal overlaps with the first two. For how can one improve the quality of instruction and respond creatively to identifiable interest groups without at the same time serving these types of students? The only difference is in terms of the motivational dimension. This goal is achieved by focusing on student needs other than those connected with the three R's. One good example of this is the Skyline Career Development Center in Dallas, whose original thrust was improving the status of "vocational education." It offered, and still does, what one educator in Dallas has termed "a whole pharmacy of educational prescriptions." In addition, it serves both the student who wants to go right to work upon graduation, and the one who wants to go directly to Harvard, Yale, Cal Tech, or Rice University. In fact, it is not necessary for a student to decide in which direction he wants to go until very late in his or her educational program. At Skyline, the doors are never closed either to a change in orientation or to an expanded interest.

Many other examples of alternatives organized to meet the needs of a specific set of students could be pointed to. So long as they are organized with this goal in mind, they will have a difficult time failing. The community of interest that results when teachers, parents, and students *voluntarily* work together in a special school almost always results in more satisfied teachers, more supportive parents, and more happy and productive children.

A story may help here to bring this point home. Cincinnati is a monolingual city; *i.e.*, everyone speaks English and, with few exceptions, only English. Yet at the same time, Cincinnati has perhaps the most rapidly growing bilingual alternative programs in the nation. Why?

One possible reason for this is that many people in Cincinnati are of German origin and, although the German language was outlawed at school by board policy during the 40's, they would like to recapture some of their lost heritage. In any case, the German-English Bilingual Program is one of the most popular in Cincinnati and now extends to grade four, with a grade being added each year as new first graders enter the program. Ultimately, it will go all the way through grade twelve. As for the teachers, they were recruited directly from Germany.

Last year, when the program extended only to grade three, Parent Night was held in one of the school auditoriums. At that time, 300 children were enrolled in the program. Yet more than 900 "parents" came to the event. If only the true parents had come, there would, of course, have been a maximum of 600. The "ringers" were grandparents, uncles, aunts, neighbors, brothers, sisters, and so forth. Never before in Cincinnati had we witnessed such a community of interest. In fact, anyone trying to dissolve that program would have had a riot on his hands.

Goal four, you will remember, is to reduce racial isolation within the school system through voluntary means. In this connection, Judge George Edwards of the Sixth Circuit Court of Appeals said only recently that "No court...to my knowledge has rejected alternative schools designed to fit particular needs of particular students without regard to race."[9] Alternative schools alone may not be sufficient, of course, to desegregate a large urban school system. But they can accomplish so much that any mandatory plan handed down is much easier to implement in a city that already has alternatives. For this reason, in city after city alternative schools are being used to reduce racial isolation. Minneapolis and St. Paul started early and have made great progress. Cincinnati's alternatives are fifty-fifty black/white, as are those in St. Louis.

Mandatory desegregation plans in small cities have quite often worked well; in larger cities, however, they have tended to accelerate the rush to the suburbs, as well as to private and parochial schools. White flight has been occurring anyway; but mandatory desegregation plans have made what might have occurred in ten years to occur in three or four. I would therefore suggest the following: do not think you will be allowed to remain segregated when, all around you, everyone is being forced to meet Constitutional requirements. Instead, act now. Don't wait. Begin your alternative system now. Give your parents and students a choice. Control the racial mix at the receiving school, but allow anyone in the district to make application to attend. And, if you run out of spots, start another alternative school.

Judge Edwards said something else recently that I think is relevant here:

> *How could we, if we wanted to, create a more dangerous condition than this – the downtown district owned by whites and occupied by them by the thousands upon thousands in daytime hours – all the rest of the central city occupied by black residents – the central city surrounded by a white suburban ring in a state dominated by whites. If you add a large white majority of policemen, firemen, and school teachers dealing with crime and fires and children in black neighborhoods, while black youth in the central city has the highest percentage of unemployment in America, such a picture presents a certainty of race conflict. Indeed, it may come to threaten domestic conflict comparable to a second Civil War.*[10]

Admittedly, the schools cannot solve all the problems of racial conflict, but in most cities they can do more than they are now doing. Children these days are in school six hours a day, five days a week. If these children are attending schools they want to attend within an integrated setting, the possibilities of reducing racial conflict are considerable. In Cincinnati, for example, no racial conflict to my knowledge has occurred in the alternative schools; in fact, virtually no discipline problems exist. For the most part, the schools are more than desegregated; they are integrated. Students, black and white, are too busy working together on tasks that interest them to have time for conflict. If you doubt me, go visit them yourselves. Do not announce your visit. Just pop in — the way parents, administrators, and others have been doing for the past four years.

You see, I believe in integration, real integration, and I want to minimize re-segregation. Alternative schools, in my view, are the best way to achieve this. If one starts in the elementary grades and allows the programs to grow one grade at a time, one will find that almost all the children remain. Why should they leave? The programs are better for them, and they are integrated. Cincinnati started with three programs. They now number twenty-one, and are found in more than forty locations. St. Louis started with nine, Minneapolis with four, and, hear this: Seattle has thirty-one planned for next September, though many of the thirty-one are duplicates at different grade levels. Seattle has done some excellent planning, and I expect to see most of them operational by the first day of school.

As for Cincinnati, it anticipates that, by 1980, forty percent of its students will be in alternative schools. Add to this the voluntary majority-to-minority transfers and the integrated neighborhoods, and the possibility that most of the city's schools can be *voluntarily* integrated becomes a potential reality.

The last goal of alternatives is to maintain a middle-income constituency in the city. This goal applies, for the most part, only to cities, while all the previous goals apply almost equally to urban, suburban, and rural school districts. Cities, as you know, are becoming increasingly black and poor. Middle-income and high-income citizens, both minority and majority, are leaving the middle city and moving into the affluent areas which now ring virtually all our major urban areas. Why do most of them leave? Because of the way they view the public school system. They see the city schools as unsafe; they think the suburban systems are better and more responsive to the needs of their children. Among other things they point to higher achievement test scores among the affluent. So what else is new?

City schools have advantages which can never be duplicated in smaller districts; the converse is true also. Smaller districts allow one child to do everything; he or she can play in the band, participate in athletics, and enter the interscholastic typing contest. City districts, on the other hand, can specialize to a degree not possible in the one, two, or eight building district. No small district could possibly afford a Skyline Career Development Center. Nor could it possibly develop a school comparable to the Creative and Performing Arts School in Cincinnati, nor offer Russian, Swahili, or Chinese. Small districts can offer alternatives, yes, but not in the number and variety of the large district.

What I am trying to say here is that city systems should take more advantage of their largeness; they should provide the diverse offerings that will attract middle-income citizens — black, white, and brown — into the school system. The migration out of the city must be reversed, and new citizens to an area must *choose* to live in the city *because* of the public school system. In Cincinnati, approximately 2,500 students have returned to the public schools from private and parochial schools during the past two years. More than one hundred are paying $850 tuition to send their children from suburban districts to one of the city's alternative schools. Many families have moved back into the city in order that their children can attend the Montessori alternative, the Math-Science Academy, the Fundamental School, or the Creative and Performing Arts School. Until recently, Montessori education was restricted to the private sector. Two years ago, however, the first public Montessori school in the nation opened in Cincinnati. This year, one opened in Dallas. Now, all over the nation, cities are planning for the initiation of Montessori schools in their districts.

Mario Fantini has put it succinctly: "Rather than looking at the negative side of urban schools, why not emphasize the positive aspects of city life? This is a process which is deceptively simple and which will require considerable planning."[11]

The rich resources of the city make almost any type of school a possibility. Our task now is to use these resources and to begin to create adequate options to meet the needs of a diverse population. Though we may need to call in consultants to help us get started, above all, let us get started *now*.

Whether you find yourself in a large, medium-sized, or small district; whether your district is wealthy or poor; whether you serve a predominantly liberal or conservative constituency—you will improve the quality of education, respond to identifiable interest groups, better serve students of varying needs, and reduce racial isolation by organizing a system of options for students and parents.

Who needs alternative schools? You do; I do; our country does. The decision to become a part of this rapidly growing development just might be the most important decision facing public schools today.

Reference Notes

Chapter 1: History and Philosophy of Alternative Schools

1. Allen Graubard, *Free the Children: Radical Reform and the Free School Movement* (New York: Pantheon Books, A Division of Random House, 1972).

2. John Bremer and Michael Von Moschzisker, *The School Without Walls: Philadelphia Parkway Program* (New York: Holt, Rinehart and Winston, Inc., 1971).

3. California Assembly Bill No. 1052, introduced by Assemblymen Dunlop, Dixon, and Vasconcellos (April 3, 1973).

4. Mario D. Fantini, "Alternative Educational Programs: Promise or Problems?" *Educational Leadership* (November, 1974), p. 86.

5. Fantini, "Educational Alternatives: Development Processes and Programs," *Options and Choice in Education* (National Commission for Citizens in Education, n.d.), pp. 45-46.

6. Fantini, "Alternative Learning Environments Based on Community Resources," Paper presented at conference at Texas A & M (Spring, 1976).

7. *Ibid.*

8. *Ibid.*

9. Fantini, "Educational Alternatives...,"p. 46.

10. Taken, with minor editorial revisions, from a news release for the Dallas Independent School District (3700 Ross Avenue, Dallas, Texas, n.d.).

11. Fantini, "Alternative Learning Environments..."

12. *Ibid.*

13. *Ibid.*

14. *Ibid.*

15. *Ibid.*

Chapter 4: Alternatives: Strategies for Getting Started

1. John B. Davis, Jr., "A Case Study: Change in a Big City School District," *Journal of Teacher Education* (Spring, 1975), p. 47.

2. Larry Reynolds et al., *Implementing Alternative Schools: Lessons from the Minneapolis Experience*. Final report submitted to NIE by Educational Services Group, Inc., pursuant to Contract No. 400-76-005, (August, 1976), pp. 1, 50, 129.

3. *Profiles of Performance in the Minneapolis Public Schools: A School-by-School Report on the Aspect of the City Testing Program and Related Factors for the 1975-76 School Year* (Minneapolis: Minneapolis Public Schools, December, 1976).

4. Seymour B. Sarason, *The Culture of the School and the Problem of Change* (Boston: Allyn and Bacon, Inc., 1971), p. 213.

5. *Ibid.*, pp. 217-218.

6. Davis, "A Case Study...," p. 47.

7. Sarason, *The Culture of the School...*, p. 222.

8. *Southeast Alternatives, Experimental Schools Program* (Minneapolis: Minneapolis Public Schools, May, 1971), pp. 3, 4, 25-28.

9. Mario D. Fantini, *Public Schools of Choice* (New York: Simon and Schuster, 1973), pp. 44-45.

10. Mary Jane Higley et al., *Progress Toward the Development of Educational Alternatives: First Semi-annual Report to the Board of Education* (Minneapolis: Minneapolis Public Schools, October, 1973), Appendix 3.

11. Higley, *Progress Toward the Development of Educational Alternatives: Second Semi-annual Report to the Board of Education* (Minneapolis: Minneapolis Public Schools, April, 1974), p. 20.

12. *Providing Optional Learning Environments in New York State Schools* (Albany, New York: The State Education Department, October, 1973).

13. Special School District No. 1, Minneapolis, Minnesota, "Policies — Bylaws — Regulations," Policy 6120, Educational Choices, adopted December 16, 1975.

14. Anthony J. Morley, *Southeast Alternatives Final Report 1971-76* (Minneapolis: Minneapolis Public Schools, 1976) p. 20.

15. *Ibid.*, p. 16.

16. Higley, *Progress Toward the Development of Educational Alternatives: Third Semi-annual Report to the Board of Education* (Minneapolis: Minneapolis Public Schools, October, 1974), p. 4.

17. Morley, "Southeast Alternatives...," appendix.

18. Reynolds, *Implementing Alternative Schools...*, p. 27

19. *Ibid.*, p. 28.

20. Roy Almen et al., *Study of Southeast Alternatives Transfer Students: Fall 1974*, (Minneapolis: Minneapolis Public Schools, 1974), pp. 21-23.

21. T. Kocher, *1974-75 Study of Elementary Student Characteristics* (Minneapolis: Minneapolis Public Schools, December, 1975), p. 5.

22. Larry Johnson, "Preferences for Educational Alternatives Expressed by Parents of Students in Minneapolis West Area Schools," *MPS Research Report #145* (Minneapolis: Minneapolis Public Schools, January, 1975).

23. *Southeast Alternatives Proposal* (Minneapolis: Minneapolis Public Schools, April, 1973), pp. 14-15.

24. *Ibid.*

25. Reynolds, *Implementing Alternative Schools...*, pp. 42-43.

26. *Ibid.*, p. 51.

27. *Ibid.*, p. 53.

28. John B. Davis, "The Teacher Center as a Strategy for Educational Renewal," Address before the National Institute of Education Panel at the AASA Convention (Dallas, Texas, Feb. 24, 1975).

29. Sarason, *Culture of the School*, p. 232.

30. Reynolds, *Implementing Alternative Schools...*," p. 34.

31. "The Southeast Alternatives Internal Evaluation Team List of Publications and Microfiche Index" (Minneapolis Public Schools, July, 1976).

32. Reynolds, *Implementing Alternative Schools...*, p. 39.

33. Higley, *Progress Toward the Development...* (April, 1974), p. 8.

34. Rodney M. French, "Financing Alternatives in Education," Address at National Institute of Education Conference on Policy Problems in Connection with Educational Options (Chicago, Illinois, June 29, 1976).

35. Reynolds, *Implementing Alternative Schools...*, p. 133.

36. "Equal Education for the Poor," *Minneapolis Tribune* (March 15, 1968). "Exploring in the School System," *Minneapolis Tribune* (October 19, 1971).

37. John B. Davis, Jr., "SEA Impact on Minneapolis Public Schools," *SEA Journal, 1971-1976* (Minneapolis Public Schools, 1975), p. 115.

38. *Ibid.*, p. 116.

39. Reynolds, *Implementing Alternative Schools...*, p. 57.

40. "Resolution to the National Institute of Education on the Southeast Alternatives Project," *Board Minutes* (Minneapolis Board of Education, Sept. 28, 1976), p. 342.

Epilogue

1. Donald R. Waldrip, "Urban Education: The Spring of Hope," *Cincinnati Chamber of Commerce Publication*, September, 1972

2. Donald Waldrip and Edgar J. Lotspeich, "Alternative Schools: Program Marketing and Student Recruitment" (First Annual International Conference on Magnet Schools, Dallas, Texas, 1977).*

3. *Ibid.*

4. *Ibid.*

5. Mario D. Fantini, "History and Philosophy of Alternative Schools" (Conference on Magnet Schools, Dallas, Texas, 1977).*

6. *Ibid.*

7. Vernon H. Smith, "Educational Options: What's Happening Today " (Conference on Magnet Schools, Dallas, Texas, 1977).*

8. Waldrip, "Schools That May Rescue Cities — As Well As Kids," *Cincinnati Magazine*, Spring, 1976.

9. George Edwards, "Legal Implications of Magnet Schools " (Conference on Magnet Schools, Dallas, Texas, 1977).*

10. *Ibid.*

11. Fantini, "History and Philosophy..."

*This speech appears in edited form as a part of this volume.

Bibliography

Chapter 5: Magnet Schools from the Student and Parent Perspective

Abramson, Paul. "Alternative Schools; They're the Rage, and a Reasonable One. How One Public School District Offers a Variety of Alternative Programs." *American School Board Journal,* Vol. 162, Number 10 (October, 1975).

Barr, Robert D. *The Growth of Alternative Public Schools: The 1975 ICOPE Report. Bloomington, Indiana: International Consortium for Options in Public Education, 1975.*

Brandstetter, John, and Charles R. Foster. "Quality Integrated Education in Houston's Magnet Schools." *Phi Delta Kappan*, Vol. 57, No. 8 (April, 1976).

Brown v. Board of Education. 347 U.S. 483 (1954).

Brown v. Board of Education. 349 U.S. 294 (1955).

Chase, Francis S., and Marjorie Buchanan. "Appraisal of Progress in Implementing the Concepts of Magnet High Schools in the Dallas Independent School District." Unpublished report. Dallas, Texas (February, 1977).

Cubberley, Ellwood P. *Public Education in the United States.* Boston: Houghton-Mifflin, 1919.

Democratic Party Platform, 1976. "A Contract with the People." *The Congressional Quarterly.* July 17, 1976.

Dunn, Rita, and Kenneth Dunn. "Learning Style as a Criterion for Placement in Alternative Programs." *Phi Delta Kappan,* Vol. 56, No. 4 (December, 1974).

Elliott, Edward C. "The Genesis of American Secondary Schools in Their Relation to the Life of the People." *National Society for the Scientific Study of Education, Fourth Yearbook.* Chicago: University of Chicago Press, 1905.

Fantini, Mario. "Education by Choice." *National Association of Secondary School Principals Bulletin,* Vol. 57, No. 374 (September, 1973).

———. "The Reform of Urban Schools." *National Education Association Center for the Study of Instruction.* Washington, D.C., 1970.

Finkelstein, Leonard B. "Alternative Schools — Choices That Can Make A Difference." *Planning and Changing,* Vol. 7, No. 1 (Spring, 1976).

Krug, Edward A. *The Shaping of the American High School.* New York: Harper and Row, 1964.

Oregon School Study Council. "Alternative Education: An Introduction, A Special Report on Pasadena, California, and a Bibliography." *Bulletin*, Vol. 17, No. 10 (June, 1974).

Sizer, Theodore Ryland. "Education and Assimilation: A Fresh Plea for Pluralism." *Phi Delta Kappan,* Vol. 58, No. 1 (September, 1976).

Smith, Vernon H., Daniel J. Burke, and Robert D. Barr. "A Description of Optional Alternative Public Schools." *Notre Dame Journal of Education,* Vol. 6, No. 4 (Winter, 1975).

Swann v. Charlotte-Mecklenburg. 402 U.S. 1 (1971).

Tasby v. Estes. 517 F. 2d 92 (5th Circuit, 1975).

The Council of Great City Schools. Unpublished policy position paper. Chicago: 1976.

Tyack, David B. *The One Best System*. Cambridge: Harvard University Press, 1974.

Chapter 8: Educational Options: What's Happening Today?

Berger, Michael. *Violence in the Schools: Causes and Remedies*. Phi Delta Kappa, 1974.

Bremer, John, and Michael von Moschzisker. *The School Without Walls: Philadelphia's Parkway Program*. New York: Holt, Rinehart, and Winston, 1971.

California State Department of Education (Sacramento). *A Report on Conflict & Violence in California's High Schools*. 1973.

Commission on Schools. *Policies and Standards for the Approval of Optional Schools and Special Function Schools*. Chicago: North Central Association, 1974.

Commission on the Reform of Secondary Education. *The Reform of Secondary Education*. New York: McGraw-Hill, 1973.

Fantini, Mario. *Alternative Education: A Source Book for Parents, Teachers, Students, and Administrators*. New York: Doubleday, 1976.

———. *Public Schools of Choice: A Plan for the Reform of American Education*. New York: Simon and Schuster, 1973.

Gibbons, Maurice. *The New Secondary Education: A Phi Delta Kappa Task Force Report*. Bloomington, Indiana: Phi Delta Kappa, 1976.

Glatthorn, Allan. *Alternatives in Education: Schools and Programs*. New York: Dodd, Mead, 1975.

Levine, Daniel, and Connie Moore. "Magnet Schools in a Big-City Desegregation Plan." *Phi Delta Kappan*, 57:8, April, 1976.

Matters of Choice: A Ford Foundation Report on Alternative Schools. 1974.

National Commission on Resources for Youth. *New Roles for Youth in the School and the Community*. New York: Citation, 1974.

National Panel on High Schools and Adolescent Education. *The Education of Adolescents*. Health, Education and Welfare Publication No. (OE) 76-00004, 1976.

National School Boards Association. *Research Report: Alternative Schools*. Evanston, Ill.: NSBA, 1976.

Neill, Shirley Boes. *Violence and Vandalism*. Arlington, Va.: Education U.S.A. Special Report, 1975.

Panel on Youth of the President's Science Advisory Committee. *Youth Transition to Adulthood*. Chicago: University of Chicago Press, 1974.

Postman, Neil, and Charles Weingartner. *The Soft Revolution*. New York: Dell, 1971.

Pursell, William. *A Conservative Alternative School: The A+ School in Cupertino*. Bloomington, Indiana: Phi Delta Kappa, 1976.

Santora, Ronald, and Louise Jensen "Reality Therapy in Reading: It's What's in People That Counts," *English Journal*, 63:8, November 1974.

Schrag, Peter, and Diane Divoky. *The Myth of the Hyperactive Child*. New York: Dell, 1975.

———. "Learning Disabilities: Education's Newest Growth Industry?" *The National Elementary Principal*, 55:4, March-April, 1976.

Smith, Vernon, Robert Barr, and Daniel Burke. *Alternatives in Education: Freedom To Choose*. Bloomington, Indiana: Phi Delta Kappa, 1976.

Smith, Vernon. *Alternative Schools: The Development of Options in Public Education.* Lincoln, Nebraska: Professional Educators Publications, 1974.

Smith, Vernon, and Robert Barr. "Where Should Learning Take Place?" *NSSE Seventy-Fifth Yearbook*, Part II, Chapter 7, 1976.

Task Force '74. *The Adolescent, Other Citizens and Their High Schools.* New York: McGraw-Hill, 1975.

U.S. Senate Subcommittee to Investigate Juvenile Delinquency. *Our Nation's Schools – A Report Card: "A" in School Violence and Vandalism*, 1975.

White House Conference on Children. *Report to the President*, 1972.